MASTERING THE GAME

MASTERING THE GAME

Strategies for Career Success

SHARON E. JONES
WITH SUDHEER R. POLURU

ISBN-13: 9780999879207
ISBN-10: 0999879200
Library of Congress Control Number: 2018901832
Drum Major Press, Chicago, IL

CONTENTS

INTRODUCTION

One day, I sat down to play a game with Liz, my nine-year-old niece. I wasn't familiar with the game since it was one she and her friends at school had created. She quickly explained some of the rules to me, and we began to play Liz's game. Every time I thought I had won the game, Liz would explain a new rule to me that she had neglected to explain at the outset. Based on that new rule, I didn't win the game. So we continued to play, and each time I thought I was winning, Liz shared a new rule. Finally, I realized that I could never win this game because I didn't understand the rules. Not knowing the rules put me at a severe disadvantage because I was never able to develop a good strategy to win.

This story is a good example of what it is like to work in most Fortune 500 corporations, U.S. government offices, and professional services firms. These organizations were created by White men and are still dominated by White men. It's no surprise that the cultural rules of these workplaces are based on the cultural norms of the dominant group that created them. Consequently, women and people of color[1] have little chance of success without a clear understanding of the rules that govern

---

1 As used throughout, the term *people of color* refers to members of racial and ethnic minority groups.

these organizations. Just as with Liz's game, it's hard to win when you don't know all the rules.

This book is designed to level the playing field for diverse professionals. Throughout this book, I use *diverse*[2] to refer to women and people of color. By standing out from the majority (White males), these groups face additional challenges in navigating the workplace culture in a variety of professional fields. These groups are not mutually exclusive, meaning that individuals can belong to more than one of them (e.g., a woman of color). *Intersectionality* is the idea that an individual's identity is best understood as a complex, interwoven relationship among all the groups to which they belong. The more aspects of your identity that stand out from the majority (White heterosexual able male), the more challenging your path will be.

This book provides the foundational rules for these organizations and gives you operational strategies for successfully playing the game at any job. Remember, the rules are the same regardless of where you work. They are the same because they are based on White male cultural norms, and those norms are carried with White males wherever they have dominated the culture. Since White males have been the dominant group creating cultural norms in the United States, these rules are at play in most sectors in the country.

I learned the rules the hard way—through trial and error and from several White male bosses who were the "Masters of the Game." I moved from job to job looking for a better workplace where the rules didn't apply. Finally, after going from law firms to government to corporate offices to not-for-profit organizations, I realized that although the substantive work varies, the rules are the same. Once I figured that out, I began to play the game by these rules to achieve the professional success

---

2 There are many dimensions of diversity. Diversity used in a broad sense refers to race, ethnicity, national origin, gender, gender identity, gender expression, religion, sexual orientation, age and/or disability. In this book, as used throughout, the term diverse is used to refer to women and racial and ethnic minorities.

I wanted. By getting a firm grasp of these unwritten rules, you will create a strong foundation for professional success. And once you master the game, you can be successful wherever you choose to work.

So where did I get these strategies for career success? They are based on my experience working in a variety of professional settings: both small and large law firms, Fortune 500 corporations, and the federal government. They are also based on research that addresses the challenges women and minorities face in ascending to leadership roles in organizations created and dominated by White males. Finally, they are based on conversations with a number of diverse and highly successful people.

One cautionary note that I want to give you is to be certain, as you move into senior leadership roles, that you do not internalize these rules. My ultimate goal is to get more diverse people in leadership roles and to transform workplace cultures to be more diverse and inclusive. The only way that will happen is to get more diverse leaders who are willing to be change agents as they move into senior leadership roles. Remember not to replicate the White male–dominated cultural norms as you move into leadership positions with the power and influence to change the rules.

The second cautionary note deals with being your authentic self. Each of you must determine what aspects of your identity and personality are essential for you to share with your coworkers in order to feel that you are authentic. You will never bring 100 percent of your identity to the office, but a significant percentage of your authentic self needs to be there in order for you to feel included and engaged. By setting forth these dominant cultural norms, it is my intention that you will understand these unwritten rules and consciously decide whether to follow them or not—recognizing that consequences will flow from each rule you decide not to follow. Only you can decide how important a particular aspect of your authentic self is to you. If your current workplace cannot accommodate your authenticity, then it isn't the best place for you. This book is useful for people who feel stuck but don't know why they are stuck.

The next chapter lays out the playing field so you will have some information about the diversity of the employers for which you may work. It also discusses a couple of psychological arguments that people often assert to hold women and other diverse professionals back: tokenism and stigma. Then it discusses how unconscious bias affects the careers of women and racial and ethnic minorities. Finally, the book sets forth 10 rules and countless strategies for career success. You can read the rules out of order, or you can go through them sequentially. There are operational strategies throughout each section and additional resources for further study. The end of the book summarizes the strategies for ease of use.

This book is for anyone who has ever felt marginalized in his or her organization for any reason. This book is for anyone who has felt unappreciated or undervalued in the workplace. And this book is for anyone who has settled for less because he or she didn't believe his or her dreams were possible. Given all the noisy signals in life, you may have lost touch with some fundamental truths. You matter. You are a value-added player. And you can achieve anything that you can dream.

So as I learned from playing with Liz, it's hard to win if you don't know the rules in advance. This book tells you the rules. Now, let's start playing to win![3]

---

3 Throughout the book, I share anecdotes based on real events as I perceived them or as they were conveyed to me. All names have been changed to respect the privacy of third parties included in the anecdotes.

THE PLAYING FIELD

The playing field refers to the diversity of the industry sector in which you are working—with a particular lens on the diversity in leadership roles. Below, I share some detailed diversity information regarding the legal, corporate, medical, and technology sectors. Regardless of the industry, you will find that women and people of color are underrepresented when compared to population demographics in the United States, which are a good benchmark when you want to track the progress of diversity initiatives. According to the most recent U.S. census, the population is 50.8 percent female and 38.7 percent racial and ethnic minorities.[1] So keep these two percentages in mind as you go through the demographic breakdowns for the legal, corporate, medical, and technology sectors. In particular, as you look at the leadership of these sectors, you often find fewer women and racial and ethnic minorities as you approach the top of these pyramids. As you read the layout of the playing field, do not be discouraged. The rules and the strategies presented in this book are designed to level the playing field and to help you reach the top leadership roles in these various sectors. Once you are in a leadership role, you can create a workplace culture that is based on multicultural norms and is more inclusive.

THE LEGAL SECTOR

In September 2017, Supreme Court Justice Ruth Bader Ginsburg recounted an instance in which she confronted unconscious bias head on. During an oral argument in the 1990s, Justice Ginsburg inadvertently interrupted Justice Sandra Day O'Connor. The headline the very next day read, "Rude Ruth Interrupts Sandra." When Justice Ginsburg went to apologize, Justice O'Connor said to think nothing of it and that the men did it all the time without apologizing. When confronted by a reporter about her manners, Justice Ginsburg told the reporter to watch how often her male colleagues interrupted their fellow justices. A month later, the reporter followed up with Justice Ginsburg and remarked that the male Justices interrupted one another all the time, but he had never noticed.[2]

Gender norms dictate that while it is OK for men to be direct and aggressive, women should be more reserved and polite. In the anecdote above, the male Supreme Court Justices were given a pass for their behavior, while the female Supreme Court Justices were judged more critically for the same behavior. This double standard applied to the behavior of women and other diverse professionals often puts them at a disadvantage as they attempt to demonstrate leadership qualities.

Although the legal profession has made progress in terms of gender, racial, and ethnic diversity, there is still a long way to go. According to the 2017 Current Population Survey conducted by the Bureau of Labor Statistics, 37.4 percent of all lawyers were women, and 14.8 percent were people of color.[3] These percentages demonstrate that the legal profession is significantly out of step with U.S. population demographics.

According to the most recent census, the U.S. population is split roughly 50-50 between males and females. In Figure 1.1, you can see that the demographics of law firm associates almost resemble the U.S. population in terms of gender. At the partner level, however, there is a huge dearth of female partners. Are women incapable of doing what partners do? Are women uninterested in becoming partners at their firms? Or are there barriers to the advancement of women? Leveling the playing field for women in law firms will require management effort to increase gender diversity at the highest levels.

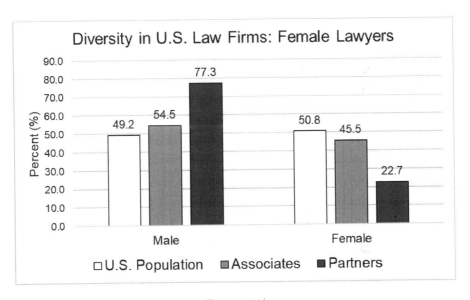

Figure 1.1[4]

What about associates of color? Do they become partners at the same rate as their White counterparts? Let's take a deeper dive into the demographic breakdown of lawyers of color. The National Association for Law Placement (NALP) 2017 Report on Diversity published data for three groups: Asians, Black/African Americans, and Hispanics.

In Figure 1.2, it is easy to see that all three groups are underrepresented in the legal sector, aside from the one bright spot of Asians being better represented at the associate level (11.4 percent). Lawyers of color are especially underrepresented at the partner level, where the numbers are dismally low, especially for Black/African American lawyers (1.8 percent) and Hispanic lawyers (2.4 percent). Once again, we ask: Are people of color incapable of performing the duties of law firm partners? Are they uninterested in the field of law and rising to positions of power and influence? Or are there barriers that create an uneven playing field for lawyers of color?

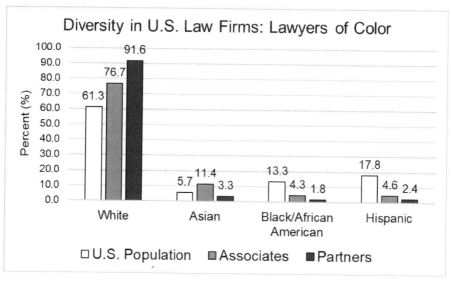

Figure 1.2[5]

If you work in the legal sector, especially in the corporate world, General Counsel (GC) is typically considered the top legal job. Each organization in the Fortune 500, the five hundred largest corporations ranked by annual revenue, has a GC heading its legal department.

What is the demographic breakdown of those 500 GCs in absolute numbers?

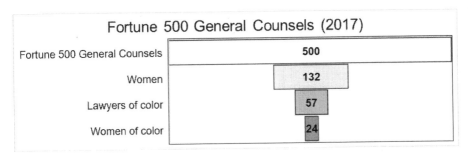

Figure 1.3[6]

Figure 1.3 shows that in 2017, there were 132 women GCs at Fortune 500 companies. At 26.4 percent, that is just over a quarter of all Fortune 500 GCs. If you think that is a high number, keep in mind that women make up more than half the U.S. population and a little over a third of the legal profession. My view is if women are a third of the legal profession, at a minimum, they should be a third of the Fortune 500 GCs. That would mean adding an additional 35 women to the top counsel spots in the Fortune 500.

The picture is even bleaker for racial and ethnic minority GCs. There were 57 lawyers of color in the top legal job at Fortune 500 companies, about 11 percent. Considering the fact that minorities make up nearly 40 percent of the U.S. population, the Fortune 500 GCs as a whole are not representative of the overall racial and ethnic diversity of the population. Even considering that minorities account for almost 15 percent of all lawyers, an additional 18 lawyers of color would need to be appointed to achieve more equitable representation in the field. Having women and racial and ethnic minorities in the position of General Counsel at Fortune 500 companies is important because they serve as role models and counter-stereotypical examples of leaders. When young men and women see people who look like them in leadership positions, they begin to believe more strongly that they, too, can become leaders, and others will see them that way.

Overall, the legal profession is becoming more diverse. People used to say that improvement was occurring at a glacial pace because before global warming, *glacial* used to mean *slow*. I don't know what the term would be now, but let's acknowledge that the pace of improvement is very slow.

THE CORPORATE SECTOR

In January 2017, Ursula Burns stepped down from her post as the CEO of Xerox Corporation.[7] In October of that year, Kenneth Chenault, the CEO of American Express, announced his upcoming retirement in early 2018. It is not uncommon for leadership in top companies to change. Both these instances, however, stand out as particularly striking because Burns was the first and, to date, the only Black woman to serve as a Fortune 500 CEO, and Chenault was one of just four Black men at the helm of a Fortune 500 company. In the history of the Fortune 500, only fourteen Black men have served as CEOs. With the departure of Burns and Chenault from the Fortune 500 executive suite, there will be no Black female CEOs and three Black male CEOs: TIAA's Roger Ferguson, Merck's Kenneth Frazier, and J.C. Penney's Marvin Ellison.[8] These three men represent less than 1 percent of all Fortune 500 CEOs.

Hispanic men do not fare much better. Although there were 10 Hispanic men serving as Fortune 500 CEOs in 2013, that number has dropped to just 5 today.[9] They are United's Oscar Munoz, AES Corporation's Andrés Gluski, ADP's Carlos Rodriguez, GameStop's J. Paul Raines, and Ryder's Robert E. Sanchez. Combined, these five Hispanic men represent just 1 percent of all Fortune 500 CEOs. Regarding women, history was made in March 2017 when Geisha Williams became the first Latina ever to become the CEO of a Fortune 500 company: PG&E.[10] At the time of Williams's appointment, the only other woman of color was PepsiCo's CEO Indra Nooyi, an Indian American. In total, people of Asian heritage make up less than 2 percent of Fortune 500 CEOs. Although few in number, these Asian individuals are making a big impact in business. The list of Asian Fortune 500 CEOs includes Microsoft's Satya Nadella, PepsiCo's Indra Nooyi, and Adobe's Shantanu Narayen.[11]

Burns wasn't the only high-profile female Fortune 500 CEO to announce she was stepping down. In November 2017, Meg Whitman revealed that she would be leaving her post as the CEO of Hewlett Packard Enterprises.[12] On the brighter side, in the same month, the Fortune 500 list of female CEOs grew by one when Gail Boudreaux was named the CEO of health insurer Anthem.[13] In total, the 2017 Fortune 500 list featured thirty-two female CEOs, a significant increase from the twenty-one recorded in 2016. While a 50 percent increase in female Fortune 500 CEOs should be celebrated, women are still woefully underrepresented in this top position of corporate America. Women make up half the U.S. population, but account for just 6.4 percent of the Fortune 500 CEO positions. Furthermore, there are only two women of color in the top position: PepsiCo's Indra Nooyi (Asian—specifically, South Asian) and PG&E's CEO Geisha Williams, the first-ever Latina to appear on the Fortune 500 CEO list.[14]

SLOW PROGRESS OF BOARD DIVERSITY

Fortune 500 board diversity is marginally better, but progress in increasing diversity is slow. Deloitte recently published the *Missing Pieces Report: The 2016 Board Diversity Census of Women and Minorities on Fortune 500 Boards*. The report found that, from 2010 to 2016, there has been limited but positive diversity progress for Fortune 500 boards. The progress has been better for women than for minorities. (See Figures 2.1 and 2.2.)

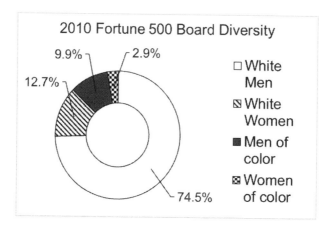

Figure 2.1[15]

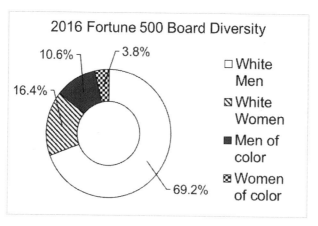

Figure 2.2[16]

In Figure 2.3, the underrepresentation of professionals of color on Fortune 500 boards is apparent. The most underrepresented group is Hispanic professionals. According to the U.S. census, Hispanics make up more than 17 percent of the U.S. population, but they are only 3.5 percent of Fortune 500 boards. On average, 8 out of every 10 Fortune 500 Board positions are held by White men and women. In order for the Fortune 500 leadership to look more like the population it serves, more professionals of color will need to occupy these positions of power and influence.

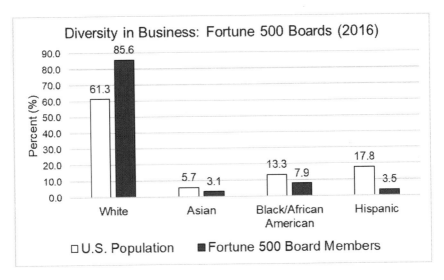

Figure 2.3[17]

In 2016, 421 independent directors were appointed to the boards of Fortune 500 companies. This total stands as a record high since the start of the Heidrick & Struggles Board Monitor report in 2009.[18] A record number of newly available board seats presented a prime opportunity to make a significant shift toward the Fortune 500 leadership mirroring population demographics in the United States. Although progress has been made, we have a long way to go before the boards of directors at Fortune 500 companies look like the diverse population of the United States.

Of all newly appointed board members, 117 were women (27.8 percent). Extrapolating from this data point, the Board Monitor report projects gender parity in board appointments to occur in 2032. This means that, at the current rate of progress, it will take more than a decade for men and women to be appointed to boards at equal rates.

Since men outnumber women four to one in board seats, it will take even longer for women to achieve equal representation on Fortune 500 boards.

The numbers for newly appointed board members of color are not much better. Of the 421 appointments, 39 were Black/African American (9.3 percent), 27 were Hispanic (6.4 percent), and 27 were Asian/Asian American (6.4 percent). The Board Monitor report does not currently collect data on other dimensions of diversity.[19]

Increasing the diversity in leadership is good for business. A 2015 McKinsey & Company report looked at the top management and boards of 366 public companies in various industries in Canada, Latin America, the United Kingdom, and the United States. McKinsey found that companies with leadership in the top quartile for gender diversity were 15 percent more likely to have financial returns above their industry median, and those in the top quartile for racial and ethnic diversity were 35 percent more likely to have financial returns above their industry median.[20] In 2018, McKinsey & Company released a follow-up report with an expanded data set. When McKinsey looked at over 1000 companies in a variety of industries across 12 countries, they once again found that greater diversity in leadership was significantly correlated to greater financial performance. Furthermore, companies with executive teams in the bottom quartile for both gender diversity and racial and ethnic diversity were 29 percent less likely to achieve above-average profitability.[21] This is important research demonstrating the potential for large financial gains to be made for companies prioritizing diversity in leadership and the possibly penalty of lagging behind financially for those companies that don't.

With research showing that companies with diverse leadership outperform companies with non-diverse leadership globally, why is progress so slow? A look at the prior experience of newly appointed board members may hold the answer. Of board members newly appointed in 2016, 50 percent were current or former CEOs, and 16 percent were current or former CFOs. Furthermore, 75 percent of newly appointed board members have previously served on boards.[22] Fortune 500 boards are selecting a vast majority of their members from a small pool of individuals who are in or have held top executive positions. This same pool of top executives features a dearth of women and professionals of color. Thus, in order to see an increase in diversity in board appointments, there need to be more diverse professionals at the top of the corporate ladder, specifically in CEO and CFO roles. Alternatively, boards could seek expertise outside the traditional CEO/CFO/board of director pools.

THE MEDICAL SECTOR

In the past few decades, great strides have been made in training more women in the medical profession. In Figure 3.1, the demographic information about current medical school students shows a nearly 50-50 split in terms of gender, closely mirroring the U.S. population. While this fact should be celebrated, there are still many unanswered questions.

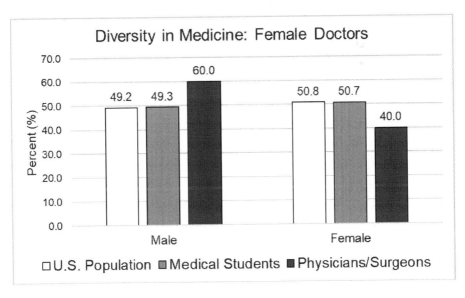

Figure 3.1[24]

For example, why are there fewer women physicians and surgeons than men? And why is there such a stark gender wage gap in the medical sector? DataUSA reports the average salary for a male physician/surgeon is $244,203 and for a female physician/surgeon is $165,305 (a difference of nearly $80,000!).[23]

As shown in Figure 3.2, when it comes to professionals of color, the medical sector is similar to the legal sector in the following way: Asians are better represented than Black/African Americans and Hispanics when compared to U.S. population demographics. It is a good sign that the demographic breakdown of physicians/surgeons closely matches that of medical school students. Even so, our work is not done. Black/African Americans and Hispanics are still underrepresented in the medical sector compared to their U.S. population demographics. The best way to move the needle forward in this situation would be to develop a pipeline of individuals from these underrepresented groups to create a push from the bottom up.

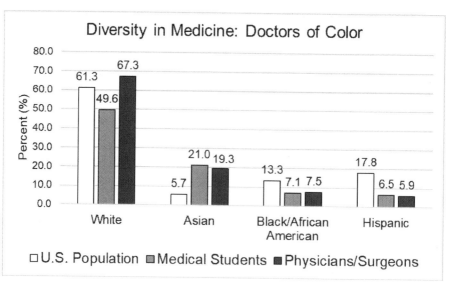

Figure 3.2[25]

THE TECH SECTOR

It seemed like the whole world turned its attention to diversity in the technology sector when an internal Google memo became public in August 2017. In what has been labeled the "Anti-Diversity Manifesto," a White male engineer expressed his belief that biological differences between men and women are the reason women are underrepresented in tech. The engineer went on to promote cognitive diversity over other types of diversity (e.g., gender, racial, ethnic, etc.).[26] The engineer was fired, and his pseudo-science claims have been debunked,[27] but we are far from finished addressing this issue.

In October 2017, the importance of cognitive diversity was brought up again by Apple's then–Vice President of Diversity and Inclusion, Denise Young Smith. Smith said she gets irritated when diversity is used to refer only to women, people of color, and people who identify as LGBT. She argued that twelve blond White men with blue eyes can be diverse, too, because of the different life perspectives they bring to the table.[28] Both statements are problematic because homogenous teams have used the notion of cognitive diversity to question the value-add of diverse populations and to keep them out of coveted career opportunities. If twelve White men bring twelve unique perspectives to the table, why should one of them be replaced by a diverse individual?

Tech companies have made a push to invest more into diversity and inclusion initiatives so their employee base can more closely reflect the population it serves. That being said, the technology industry is still predominantly composed of White males. Although progress has been made, there is still a long way to go until the Tech sector mirrors the U.S. population. Let's take a look at the numbers for women and people of color in four tech giants: Apple, Microsoft, Google, and Facebook.

GENDER DIVERSITY IN TECH

According to the U.S. census, 51 percent of the population is female. In the tech sector, women are drastically underrepresented in technical and leadership roles. *Technical* refers to those roles that require substantial knowledge of and abilities in the fields of Science, Technology, Engineering, or Math (STEM). Engineering, computer programming, and software development are all considered technical roles. Human resources and marketing would be considered nontechnical roles. The chart below shows that women fill less than a quarter of technical roles at some of the largest tech companies chosen for this sample. Prospects are a little brighter for leadership positions. Women comprise around a quarter of all leadership positions at Apple, Google, and Facebook. A recent analysis showed that Wall Street is outpacing Silicon Valley on gender equality. Female employees make up nearly half (48.4 percent) of the workforce in America's top banks, while accounting for only a third (33.2 percent) of the workforce in top technology companies. Representation of women in leadership at banks (around 25 percent), however, is no better than in the technology industry.[29]

Many companies tout their overall employee gender breakdown to show how much progress has been made incorporating women into the tech sector. Upon closer inspection, we see that women make up just about a fifth of technical roles in some of the nation's largest technology companies: Apple, Microsoft, Google, and Facebook. This trend of underrepresentation gets marginally better at the leadership level; around a quarter of leaders at the nation's largest technology companies are women. (See Figure 4.1.)

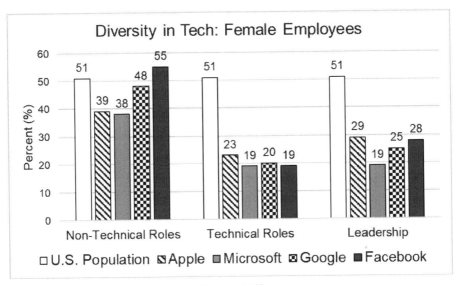

Figure 4.1[30]

RACIAL AND ETHNIC DIVERSITY IN TECH

The Asian population is overrepresented in the tech sector when compared to population demographics, with particularly strong representation in technical roles and leadership. (See Figure 4.2.)

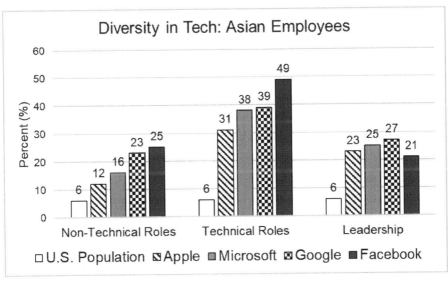

Figure 4.2[31]

Black/African American professionals are underrepresented in the tech sector, especially in technical and leadership roles. (See Figure 4.3.) Although they represent about 13 percent of the U.S. population, their representation in technical and leadership roles hovers between 1 and 3 percent. The notable exception is Apple's Black/African American representation in technical roles, which far exceeds that of its peers at 7 percent.

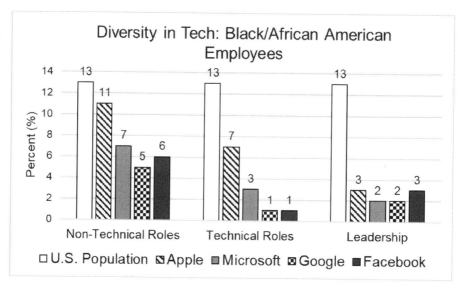

Figure 4.3[32]

Hispanic professionals are also underrepresented in the tech sector. Once again, the difference in representation becomes more stark when we look closely at technical and leadership roles. (See Figure 4.4.) While Hispanics make up about 18 percent of the U.S. population, they only make up between 2 and 4 percent of the coveted technical and leadership positions in some of the nation's largest technology companies. Although Apple leads its peers and has nearly double the percentage of Hispanic professionals in technical and leadership roles, it, too, falls short of mirroring the U.S. population.

There is still much more work to be done to increase the diversity of the tech sector.

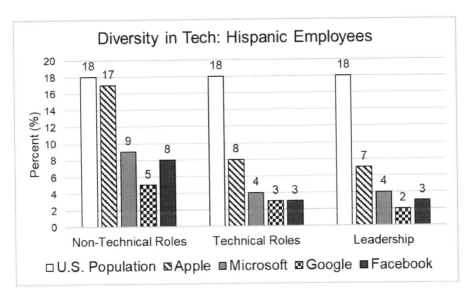

Figure 4.4

What these data tell us is that the legal, corporate, medical, and tech sectors are still very homogenous. There are several reasons for this homogeneity: 1) Diverse professionals don't know the unwritten cultural rules for success in these sectors, so they decide to leave when they are passed over for developmental and advancement opportunities; 2) negative stereotypes and unconscious bias often make it more difficult for diverse professionals to succeed; and 3) organizational structures often make it more difficult for diverse people to succeed.

THE VALUE OF DIVERSITY

By 2040 or so, it is estimated that population demographics in the United States will be over 51 percent people of color. Millennials are already more racially and ethnically diverse than previous generations. As millennials continue to move into the workforce, they will bring that diversity with them. Although racial and ethnic diversity is increasing, you still need to master the rules of the game to be successful because the rules were created by White men. As an initial matter, it is important to understand the value of diversity.

Diverse teams create better solutions to complex problems and generate greater financial returns. For a fascinating and informative read, see *The Difference: How the Power of Diversity Creates Better Groups, Firms, Schools, and Societies* by Scott E. Page. In his book, Page presents numerous studies that show how groups that display a range of perspectives consistently outperform like-minded experts on complex tasks.[33] As I noted earlier, there is a substantial positive correlation between diverse leadership teams and financial performance. For those of you whose value and credentials are constantly questioned, arm yourself with the research that shows you are undeniably a valued asset to any team. Show any doubters the research from McKinsey & Company,[34] *Scientific American*,[35] the Catalyst Information Center,[36] or the International Monetary Fund[37] quantifying the value of diversity in the workplace. Long story short: in order to operate more effectively, the workplace and work teams need to be diverse and more closely mirror population demographics.

CONSCIOUS AND UNCONSCIOUS BIAS

A big component of successfully playing the game to achieve career success is remaining in the most positive frame of mind possible in order to stay motivated and to rebuff any intentional or unintentional slights. To be as psychologically strong as possible, I recommend keeping a journal and regularly using it to clear your head of negative thoughts. You can also use the journal to frame positive thoughts in your mind before you are confronted with various scenarios. You often hear athletes say they mentally play their games over and over in their heads before they actually play them. They see themselves hitting the perfect shot over and over. That is the type of mental preparation you need to do regularly, and writing in a journal can be one way of doing so. I find that writing things down tends to burn them into my subconscious. Often when you do that, things happen just the way you imagined them.[38]

Another aspect of the psychological game is protecting yourself from negative thoughts associated with tokenism. The statistics I provided earlier suggest that, as a professional of color, you may find yourself in situations in which you are the only person of color in the room, the office, or a meeting. In some instances, you may be brought onto a team expressly to increase the diversity of that team. Many times, I have been in this situation. I think this can be a very smart thing to do, because I know that diverse teams yield better results. But I have heard people in these situations say, "I feel like a token" or "Someone suggested that I am a token." I never feel like a token because I see myself as someone adding value to the process. I encourage you to see yourself as a value-added player as opposed to a token. No one can make you a token as long as you are adding value. Don't allow someone to sabotage or diminish you by asserting that tokenism is at play.

There is lot of stigma around affirmative action. If you are a person of color, it is not uncommon for people to assume that you got your job or admission into a college or university because of affirmative action. The unstated presumption is that, as a beneficiary of affirmative action, you are somehow less qualified or less skilled than others in the applicant pool. People are trying to make you feel "less than," but you can't let this get to you. I have been the beneficiary of affirmative action. Furthermore, I will continue to be the beneficiary of any opportunity that someone wants to give me because I know that

I will deliver. I never felt stigmatized, and I never felt like a token. In many instances, I was the only person like me in the room. But that fact alone does not make someone a token. You are only a token if you don't add value. If you make valuable contributions to the project or initiative, then you are not just there for show. You were put on the team because you have something to contribute. That's where I am coming from when I say you own it; don't let someone else put that on you. Some rules are so deeply ingrained you don't even realize that you have internalized the wrong ones. Now it is time to learn the real rules.

One negative thought that often arises is the idea that diverse people are stigmatized by participating in programs and efforts to level the playing field. Minority- and women-owned business programs are examples designed to level the playing field and to match women and minorities with business opportunities connected to public-sector contracts. Mentoring and sponsorship programs are designed to provide women or other diverse professionals with mentors or sponsors, thereby initiating relationships essential to moving into leadership roles in most organizations. Sometimes I hear women or minorities say, "I don't want to participate because I will be stigmatized by my participation in this program." These programs are specifically designed to level the playing field and to reduce structural barriers within the workplace that may make it difficult for diverse people to advance. They are also designed to reduce the impact of unconscious bias, which tends to disadvantage diverse people in these homogenous White male environments.

Don't feel stigmatized by participation in a program designed to level the playing field. See yourself as the value-added player. These programs are important to advance diverse individuals into leadership roles. They also provide a safe way for White men of power and influence to support the professional development of women and people of color without being misunderstood.

Many people bring up the tokenism and stigma argument due to bias—either conscious or unconscious. Unconscious bias (sometimes referred to as implicit bias) describes the mental shortcuts that we take to process information and make decisions. These biases are informed by both our lived experiences and our lack of them. Unconscious bias can be positive or negative and explains why we tend to generally favor those in our own group. It explains why we're more willing to strike up a conversation with strangers if we learn that they graduated from our alma mater. It also helps explain why, when identical resumes are sent out, those from applicants with stereotypically White names are 50 percent more likely to receive a callback for an interview than those from applicants with stereotypically Black names.[39]

Unconscious bias, when left unchecked, is pervasive. While this barrier can seem daunting, it should also inspire some optimism. This is because unconscious bias—with awareness and intentionality—can be significantly disrupted. When we are aware of our unconscious biases, we can begin to question them. This process involves becoming aware of the biased heuristics (mental shortcuts used to offload the cognitive load of making a decision), questioning our snap judgments, and slowing down our thinking to make more thoughtful, more informed, and ultimately, better decisions. Because unconscious bias is so pervasive, a company or team that chooses to address this issue has tremendous opportunities for positive payoffs via rippling effects.

I encourage you to think about these psychological aspects carefully and be mentally prepared if anyone challenges your right to be in your position or role. Remember to visualize yourself acting self-confidently and handling your work in a first-class manner—just like the athletes practicing their game shots in their heads. It is one of the psychological secrets to success.

Nobody likes to play a game that they feel is rigged against them where they have no chance for success. So let's learn the rules and strategies, and let's start playing to win!

Rule 1

SUCCESS IS INTENTIONAL

Create your own definition of success and intentionally work to
achieve it.

*Effort and courage are not enough
without purpose and direction.*

—*JOHN F. KENNEDY*

It's not uncommon to hear a successful person say, "I don't know how I
achieved this level of success. I was just lucky, I guess." I never believe
that. There are many decisions you make in your life, both large and
small, that affect your career success. It is by approaching your career
very intentionally that you achieve the level of success you desire.

Many people don't realize how important or taxing the mental
part of the game can be. The mental game (also called the psychological game) is all about having the right mindset when you show
up to work. I will talk about the psychological game more in the next
chapter. For now, the mindset I want you to develop is that *success is*

intentional. This mindset sets the stage for all the other rules. First and foremost, recognize and acknowledge the role you play in your life. If you want to play the game, then you need to become an active participant in your life. To do so, you will need to make a marked shift away from the go-with-the-flow mindset. Begin to develop an internal attitude of control and realize just how much autonomy you have in many areas of your life. Instead of just letting life happen to you and playing the role of a victim who is at the mercy of everyone and everything around you, begin to make the types of decisions that increase the quality of your life and get you closer to achieving your vision of success. Of course, there are some things outside your control. Life is indeed unpredictable. Instead of worrying about everything that could go wrong, just focus on what you can control. The only thing you can control in your life is yourself. Coupled with this simple truth is the notion that your actions make a difference in the world. No matter how big or small, your actions have a real impact on the outcomes in your life.

You can achieve your heart's desires by focusing on what's important to you and being strategic in your decision-making. Just as in a game of chess or baseball, every choice you make matters. It is important to develop a good strategy for weighing your options and making the best decision quickly and efficiently.

TWO-STEP PROCESS

To break down the success-is-intentional mindset and how to implement it in your life, we will go through two steps. First, you must define what success means for you. Second, you have to set and meet goals that serve as stepping-stones to your definition of success. The idea is to move from abstract goals to concrete actions. Through this process, you can turn your vision into reality.

STEP 1: DEFINING SUCCESS

What does success mean to you? We often label people successful if they have wealth, fame, or power. It is very easy to take on other people's definitions of success. It is much harder to create our own vision of success independently. As human beings, we seek external validation. The concern over what people think about us can drive us to pursue superficial praise instead of deep fulfillment or worse—to pursue other people's goals for us as opposed to our own. Early in my legal career, I decided I wanted to be a General Counsel. Why? Because it was prestigious, it paid well, and it was a reasonable next step since I was already a senior in-house corporate lawyer. After two General Counsel interviews, I asked myself, "Do you really want to be a General Counsel?" The answer was no. It did pay well, but it was too much stressful, 24/7 work, and I wouldn't have had enough time to do the kind of work that made me happy. The fact that I thought I would be good at being a General Counsel made it a harder decision. Plus, other people thought I should go after that position, which added another layer to the difficulty of the decision. However, I realized that I needed to do work that made me happy and not to follow other people's definitions of success.

Similarly, a friend of mine graduated from law school and went to work in a firm. After realizing she wasn't enjoying herself, she decided to pursue a position in politics—something she loved. Eventually, she thought it was time to "get serious" and returned to a law firm. That was a very bad idea for her. She never liked the legal practice. She had no legal skill set since she hadn't practiced long enough to develop one, and she had no passion for it. Was she successful in law? No. Why did she pursue it? Because she thought it was prestigious and other people would be impressed. That should never be the reason you choose a career path. Choose one that feeds your soul!

Don't worry; we won't get overly philosophical and ponder the meaning of life in this book. I'll leave it up to you to decide what kind of life you want to lead. With every path, there are pros and cons. Following your passions to serve a not-for-profit organization may mean taking a pay cut. Accepting a demanding promotion may mean less time with family and friends. In your life, don't just react to the circumstances or limited options presented to you. Be intentional about what your idea of success looks like, and then you can take steps to figure out how to get there.

The definition of success doesn't only vary greatly from person to person. Each of our definitions is subject to change based on our circumstances in life. Your childhood goal of becoming a superhero might have changed to fitting in at your high school then later morphed into juggling the demands of personal and professional life. According to a 2013 Accenture study on job satisfaction, 70 percent of both male and female professionals around the world say they can "have it all," meaning a successful career and a full life outside work. However, 50 percent also said that they cannot "have it all at the same time."[40] Professionals continually reformulate their definitions of success over the course of their careers.

The definition of success is not constant because for many, career goals and personal priorities will take precedence at different times. Fresh out of college, a young professional without a family may have the time and energy to put in long hours. The arrival of a child or caring for a loved one in poor health may require a shift to part-time status or an unpaid leave. Sending the last child off to college may free up time to take on more responsibility at work.

PRIORITIES CHANGE OVER TIME

A study analyzed the responses of a group of sixty-six college students in the Northeast to determine how the students defined success each year in college. The sample included 73 percent women and 65 percent students of color or international students. To the question "What would make this year of college successful?" the responses illustrated that the definition of success changes depending on our circumstances and position in life. In their first year, 77 percent of students reported that grades were important in determining their success, while only 61 percent of students in their final year agreed. The students who reported that career-oriented activities mattered to them jumped dramatically from 9 percent freshmen year to 65 percent senior year. Many of us probably experienced the same shift during our time in college. As we got closer to graduation, we started thinking less about grades and much more about the next step, getting internships and job experience to be prepared to enter the workforce.

Accompanying this change in priorities was a change in the personal definitions of success. Outside the realm of academics, students had shifting priorities when it came to their social lives, too. For 56 percent of freshmen, making new friends was an important aspect of social and residential life success. That number dropped to just 3 percent senior year, while maintaining friendships grew in importance from 6 percent in year one to 42 percent in year four.[41] As we settle into our careers, we, too, may find that maintaining relationships with friends and family takes precedence over forming new bonds.

Once you are in the working world, you need to identify the various aspects of your life (e.g., friends, family, work, exercise, personal time) and the appropriate balance among them. During the course of your reflection, you may want to read *How Will You Measure Your Life?* by Clayton M. Christensen. This book made me think deeply about how to have a successful professional life, sustain a fulfilling personal life, and live a life of integrity. You may also find it helpful to engage those around you in conversation. Hearing a variety of responses, you may find that some resonate with you more than others. These conversations can serve as a good foundation for honing in on your personal concept of success.

Remember to dream big dreams as you set your goals. If you are willing to put in the time and energy, anything is possible, especially in the brainstorming phase. Don't be afraid to shoot for the moon—you might just reach it! A good example of this is President Barack Obama. Who imagined that a Black person with the name Barack Obama would become President of the United States in our lifetime? I never expected to see a Black president in my lifetime. I thought there were too many obstacles and too much racism to allow that to happen. But clearly, Barack Obama believed it was possible and intentionally made decisions consistent with that dream. So be willing to dream a big dream—regardless of the odds.

> *We don't all have to aspire to the top job just because we think we ought to; but equally we shouldn't set our sights too low, just because it's what other people expect.*
>
> —MARGARET ROBINSON[42]

THE SUCCESS-HAPPINESS CONNECTION

Of the more than two thousand Americans adults surveyed as part of the Success Project, 90 percent believed that success is defined by happiness.[43] This connection between success and happiness may exist globally. In his TED Talk, Shawn Achor, an American happiness researcher, outlined a widely accepted formula for success, which states, "If I work harder, I'll be more successful. And if I'm more successful, then I'll be happier."[44] This formula sets up an assumption about the order of events. Success comes first. Happiness comes second. This leads to the idea that our happiness is ultimately dependent on how successful we are in life.

The problem with this approach, as we identified earlier, is that we are constantly changing our definition of success. As the circumstances in our lives change and as we reach our goals, we redefine our goals and visions of success. If happiness comes after success, our happiness is an ever-moving target that we may never reach. Achor presents an alternative theory in which he argues that the true formula for success could be happiness first, then success. Studies in the field of positive psychology[45] show that your brain at positive is 31 percent more productive than your brain at negative, neutral, or stressed. This productivity boost is now known as the happiness advantage.[46] Therefore, by prioritizing happiness in the present, we allow our brains to work more efficiently, which can lead to greater success.

STEP 2: TURNING IDEAS INTO PLANS

One way to create your vision of success is to ask yourself where you want to be 5 years, 10 years, or even 20 years from now—if you know that far out. Identifying where you want to end up may be a difficult task that requires time and soul searching. Or it may be an easy task because you already think about it every single day. After identifying the end goal, think backward about steps that will get you to your destination within the allotted time. By starting with the end goal in mind, you can spend your time more efficiently and purposefully. Identifying your goal is the first half of the success equation. The second half is engaging in consistent action that gets you to your goal. These two parts can be simplified into the *what* and the *how*. First, you identify *what* you want. Then you create a plan for *how* to get it.

When thinking about what you want, make sure you create a complete picture. It is important to recognize that you cannot compartmentalize your life. Your personal and professional lives are interconnected and constantly competing for your attention. It is never too early to start thinking about your future. At what age do you want to retire? What do you want your retirement life to look like? Where do you want to live? Do you want children? Do you want to live near your friends? Do you want to live near your family or to avoid your family? Where is it important for you to live now and for the next five years? Do you need to have access to outdoor activities all the time? Are you more urban than suburban? Consider all these questions as you begin framing your goals. Remember to set a goal but to allow room for flexibility as circumstances change.

Below are a few operational strategies on visualizing a future based on your definition of success.

OPERATIONAL STRATEGIES: VISUALIZING SUCCESS

- Form a clear vision of your dream life as far out as possible (5, 10, even 20 years).
- Keep in mind both your personal and professional lives when envisioning your future. Be as detailed as possible. What is your workday like? Where do you live?

After figuring out what you want, the next step is figuring out how to get it.

SET S.M.A.R.T.E.R. GOALS

Back in November 1981, George Doran first introduced the idea of setting goals using the acronym S.M.A.R.T. A S.M.A.R.T. goal is specific, measurable, assignable, realistic, and time-related.[47] The effectiveness of S.M.A.R.T. goals goes beyond business strategy and can be applied to personal goals as well. Here is how the acronym was changed slightly to fit the framework of setting S.M.A.R.T.E.R. personal goals:[48]

- Specific—Set detailed, concrete goals, *not* abstract ones.
- Meaningful—Identify why this goal matters to you.
- Achievable—Dream big, then plan realistically given current constraints.
- Relevant—Set goals that impact a core area of your life for the better.

- Time-Bound—Define an exact date for when you want to achieve the goal.
- Evaluate—Frequently reflect on what is going well and what needs to change.
- Readjust—Change your approach as needed based on your evaluations.

When I went to law school, I knew I wanted to be a trial attorney—just like those I had seen on television. So when I got there, I *chose* to take a trial advocacy course, which gave me a chance to practice trial work as a law student. I loved that course! When I had to choose a job, I *chose* a law firm that did a lot of litigation, thinking I would have a better chance to litigate there. And it was true in a way. I got to handle a small federal court trial alone with a partner's advice. It excited me so much that I realized I wanted to try cases more often. I had a friend who worked in the U.S. Attorney's Office and loved her job. She tried cases all the time and worked for justice. I thought it was my dream job. So I *chose* to apply, was hired, and *chose* to leave the law firm to do work that fed my soul. I also got lots of trial experience, which put me in a position to do trial work later in my career. I am sharing this story to demonstrate that the choices you make can support your heart's desire or not. In going to work for the federal government, I took a pay cut, and many people thought I was crazy to leave the law firm world, when it is hard to get a job in big law firms. But I followed my heart and made the choices that both helped me achieve my goal to be a trial lawyer and fed my soul. Your choices do matter. Each choice builds on the last one to get you to your goal.

CREATE AN ACTIONABLE PLAN

Of the seven factors of S.M.A.R.T.E.R. goals, which do you think is the most important? If you guessed *S* for specific, you'd be right. A meta-analysis of goal-setting research found that specific and challenging goals overwhelmingly lead to higher performance than easy goals, do-your-best goals, or not setting any goals. There are a few reasons why goals, when set correctly, can lead to better performance. Goal setting affects performance by focusing attention, raising effort, improving persistence, and inspiring the development of different ways of achieving the goal.[49]

WRITE DOWN YOUR GOALS AND FIND A BUDDY

A study conducted at Dominican University had two interesting and informative results. First, the study found that individuals with written goals achieved more of them than individuals with unwritten goals. The study also found that individuals with written goals and commitments to provide progress updates to a friend achieved more of their goals than either those with just written goals or those with unwritten goals.[50] This study highlights the importance of accountability for achieving your goals. When you write something down, there is tangible proof that you set a goal. Giving progress reports to a friend holds you even more accountable by recruiting a third party to track your progress over time.

Below are strategies to keep in mind as you develop a concrete plan and execute it to achieve your goals.

OPERATIONAL STRATEGIES: MAKING A PLAN

- Write your goals down in as much detail as possible.
- Work backward from your end goal and identify concrete steps that serve as stepping-stones to your destination. If you don't know the steps to get there, ask your mentor or others who may know.
- Set SMARTER goals to reach each stepping-stone on your path.
- Reflect on your progress frequently, and adjust your plan of action as necessary.

- Recruit a trusted adviser, friend, or family member to call you out when you stray from your path.
- Look into apps like STICKK, a free goal-setting platform created by behavioral economists. You can either partner with someone to serve as a coach and see your progress reports or place a wager on the goal yourself. If you fail to meet your goal, the wagered money goes to a preselected charity of your choice.

CONCLUSION

Many times, we try to make sense of our lives by looking back and trying to connect the dots in hindsight. Imagine what that process would look like if we flipped it on its head. Forget about trying to formulate a meaningful story out of historical data points. Instead, start with your ideal life story, create an actionable plan to get you there, and then make decisions that align with your vision. It is easier to get to your destination if you know where you want to go.

Rule 2

MASTER THE PSYCHOLOGICAL GAME

Develop mental toughness for the road ahead. Your thoughts and
actions must be aligned.

No one can make you feel inferior without your consent.

—*ELEANOR ROOSEVELT*

Once you identify your vision of success and an actionable plan, it is
vital to be mentally prepared for obstacles, criticism, and setbacks
on your journey. The road to success can take many forms. It could be
a newly paved highway without any traffic or tolls. In my experience,
however, more than likely it will be a gravel road laden with potholes
and few street signs to let you know if you are headed in the right direction. To achieve success, you must not only believe in yourself, but also
be prepared to face all those who doubt you. In this chapter, I will cover
two psychological concepts that diverse people often face: stereotype
threat and self-fulfilling prophecy. After covering a basic explanation
of these two concepts, we will go over some operational strategies for
developing a strong mental game.

STEREOTYPE THREAT

As a diverse professional in a White male–dominated organization you need to be aware of the role that stereotypes about your race, gender, and/or sexual orientation may play in the minds of your work colleagues. Stereotype threat can occur when you feel at risk of confirming a negative stereotype attached to an aspect of your identity. In a series of studies, Claude M. Steele, PhD, and Joshua A. Aronson, PhD, administered difficult verbal reasoning tests to Black and White college students at Stanford University to investigate the effects of stereotype threat. In the control condition, without any experimental manipulations, Black and White students scored equally well on the tests. When the students were asked to report their race as part of the demographic information before the test, Black students performed worse than White students. Simply asking Black students about their race impaired their performance.[51] Why? Because there are many negative stereotypes about the intellectual ability of Black people. Other racial and ethnic minority groups also face stereotype threat when they have to combat negative stereotypes about their intellectual ability. For example, Latino men and women performed worse on math tests when told the tests were accurate measures of their abilities.[52]

Stereotype threat is damaging because stereotypes are deeply ingrained, often so subtly we hardly recognize them. Even when no one explicitly states the stereotypes that capture our so-called deficiencies, we are aware of the stereotypes associated with the demographic groups to which we belong. These negative stereotypes are always present in the backs of our minds and can have powerful effects. Unless we consciously combat them, they can potentially harm our performance.

One great example of combating stereotype threat was a study that gave participants the disclaimer that the math test they were about to take had not shown any gender differences in performance of mathematics ability. When given this disclaimer, women outperformed men. When the test was given without this disclaimer, stereotype threat was not negated, and women's performance dropped while the men's performance was unchanged.[53] In life, women, but not men, often have to deal with the negative stereotype that they are bad at math. This is only the tip of the iceberg. In today's society, women are constantly presented with messages indicating they are deficient and inferior to men in many professional aspects. Black/African American and Hispanic employees constantly have their work ethic, integrity, and competence questioned. Asian employees, while seen as hard workers, stereotypically are considered followers, not leaders. The sad thing is that, in a world without disclaimers correcting these misconceptions, women and professionals of color may perform poorly and start to believe the stereotypes are true.

Unfortunately, most stereotypes about minorities and women in the workplace are negative. If you are a professional of color working in predominantly White spaces, you should assume that most people will possess little or no real-life experience with a member of your racial group. Even in diverse societies, most people live around and predominantly interact with members of their own race. If they have had a real-life experience with a member of your racial group and it was perceived as negative, they will unconsciously project those feelings onto you because of a lack of positive experiences to counterbalance the negative one. If there is another aspect of your identity that makes you a minority member in your organization, (e.g., gender, gender identity, sexual orientation, disability status, age), then you, too, may be facing a scarcity of positive experiences associated with people in your demographic group.

It can be challenging to work under the weight of these crushing stereotypes. Therefore, you need to be aware of that fact and realize that you will most likely be required to prove your worth and value to your employer on numerous occasions. This phenomenon has been referred to as a rebuttable presumption of incompetence. In the old days, there was an irrebuttable presumption of incompetence. No matter what you tried, you would not be able to persuade your coworkers and superiors that you were a competent, hardworking individual, let alone vital to the success of the company. Now, the presumption is rebuttable. You can persuade them that you are competent, but it will take some time and a great deal of effort on your part. The fact that you have to prove your competence is unfair, but at least you get the opportunity to do so, unlike your ancestors. The rules that follow are some of the keys to showing you how to play the game to not just survive but thrive in organizations where you may feel undervalued or marginalized.

SELF-FULFILLING PROPHECY

Whether someone subtly questions your effectiveness as a leader or explicitly attacks your ability to complete a difficult task, he or she may be viewing your behavior through the lens of the negative stereotypes associated with your identity as a woman or person of color. In these instances, it is important to remain mentally tough and not fall prey to stereotype threat. If you begin to buy in to these negative stereotypes, you may begin to doubt yourself. As a result, your performance may be hindered, which can lead you down the spiral to a self-fulfilling prophecy of failure.

I faced a stereotype threat from a supervisor once. I had a written project to do as part of a group, and we were using a template for the written materials. We just needed to change the names and the facts, and basically, the indictment and supporting memorandum would be ready to go. When I turned it in, my supervisor told me it was poorly written. When I asked him what was wrong, he told me to ask my peer, Mark, what was wrong with it. Mark was my friend and leading this project, so I asked him. He said nothing was wrong: "You followed my format, and that was what you were supposed to do." I edited the memorandum in a minor way and turned it back in with no problems. You should know that I assumed my supervisor was reacting to a stereotype of "Blacks can't write" from the moment he said my memorandum was poorly written. I knew it because I followed closely the format that Mark had given me. I knew it was a negative stereotype because I had received awards for writing at different points in my life, and I didn't wake up that day unable to write. I knew he was relying on the stereotype because he couldn't tell me what was wrong with the memorandum. So I shrugged it off and kept moving. I did not allow his criticism to make me believe I couldn't write, and I never heard that from any supervisor in that office during the four years I was there or from any supervisor since that time. I was prepared for that mental game (i.e., people questioning my writing ability), and I didn't fall for it.

A self-fulfilling prophecy is when a person's expectations subconsciously change the way that person acts in such a way that causes his or her prediction to come true.[54] Self-fulfilling prophecies arise out of the strong connection between belief and behavior. Positive beliefs can lead to positive outcomes, and negative beliefs can lead to negative outcomes. It is up to you to reinforce positive thinking and minimize negative thinking. The smallest thoughts can have a profound impact on your performance because they change your mindset and behavior in subtle ways. In the previous chapter, I discussed the importance of believing success is intentional. If you believe building your dream is within your control, then you begin to do things that get you one step closer to your goal. And as you get closer to your goal, your belief is reinforced, and you pursue further action with greater conviction.

In this section, we are focusing on negative self-fulfilling prophecies. Small negative thoughts can also be reinforced and change our behaviors in ways that lead us to the very outcome of failure we had hoped to avoid. Negative self-talk, when our inner voice so eloquently expresses all our insecurities and doubts, can quickly spiral out of control. In addition to our own insecurities, we need to be prepared to handle people questioning our abilities. Even seemingly harmless statements can trigger a detrimental cascade of events if we aren't mentally prepared to process them.

For example, a woman is assigned to lead a project that is highly quantitative. Her boss makes a passing comment about how it is a little unusual that a woman is assigned as the project lead because of the nature of the work. The female employee is reminded of the negative stereotype that women aren't good at math. She begins to worry that she may have gotten in over her head by accepting this assignment.

The employee hits a roadblock during the project, which is no big deal; it has happened a few times before. However, instead of talking through the problem with the other members of her team, she struggles with the problem on her own. She doesn't want to ask for help because doing so, in her mind, would be admitting that she was not capable of handling the quantitative-heavy assignment. Spending longer hours working in solitude, she forgoes meals and sufficient sleep. Tired and increasingly more stressed, she begins to make errors in her work. In the end, her performance is subpar. The small changes in her behavior made her fear that she was in over her head all along a reality.

No matter what the outcome of a project is, you must acknowledge that you are more than any singular event in your life. For a strong mental game, it is important to adopt a growth mindset, as opposed to a fixed mindset. Those who have fixed mindsets believe their traits, like intelligence and talent, are innate and static. Those with growth mindsets believe traits can be developed through deliberate effort and persistence.[55] Individuals with growth mindsets embrace the notion that hard work pays off and that they are full of unrealized potential. When confronted with failure, those with fixed mindsets give up because they believe there is nothing they can do, while those with growth mindsets look for opportunities to learn from the setback and develop themselves for future challenges. The takeaway here is to believe in your untapped potential and be willing to put in the effort to develop it. Obstacles and setbacks are part of life. Instead of allowing them to halt your progress, use them as tools to grow and develop yourself further.

Below are a few strategies for developing mental toughness as you pursue your goals.

OPERATIONAL STRATEGIES: YOUR PSYCHOLOGICAL GAME

- Stay in touch with other high-performing diverse people. You need to do so to counteract the effect of the negative stereotyping that may be occurring in your work environment. By staying connected to other diverse people, you can reduce feelings of isolation. Also, the more you connect with high-achieving diverse people, the more you will be burning into your mind the belief that diverse people are high achievers. This makes you better able to brush off any negative stereotypes thrown at you. Remember, it's hard to fly like an eagle if you hang out with pigeons.

- Don't take things personally. Many of the things that happen are not based on you personally but may be directed to someone in your demographic group. If you do not take things personally, you can stay objective and strategize better. You always want to be thinking a few moves ahead, not reacting to events. If you take things personally, you are always reacting based on emotions.

- Zoom out and remember your vision. See yourself and your role at the firm or company as part of a bigger whole. You want to remind yourself of the end goal you are working toward in a way that will inspire you to continue moving forward when the going gets rough. A minor setback does not negate how far along you have come. By zooming out and putting things into perspective, you will be better equipped to handle the inevitable frustrations of the daily grind.

COME ON COACH, PLAY ME: ALWAYS ACT LIKE A WINNER

Up to this point, I have discussed the defensive aspects of the mental game. Being ready to handle negative events, comments, and stereotypes will keep you in the game longer. There is one more component that is vital to the mental game, and that is offense. Beyond just being on the defensive, you can signal that you are a high-value individual by acting like a winner. You must never forget that you are a value-added player in the equation, no matter what the situation is. You bring a unique set of experiences that no one else can offer. Too often, women and people of color are taught to dim their own light in order not to make others feel bad. By remaining in the box that others put you in, however, you do yourself a disservice. The default perception of women and professionals of color is that they are average or below-average performers. The first step is protecting yourself from allowing these negative assumptions to dominate your thinking and affect your performance. The next step is getting others to see that you are really a winner. You can challenge the assumptions that people make and the expectations they have about your abilities and performance by the way you carry yourself and behave.

SELF-DOUBT AND SELF-CONFIDENCE

Adam Grant, a business professor, took up the task of studying "Originals," successful people who not only have innovative ideas but also take action to see them through. It turns out Originals don't strike gold because of any innate differences in talent or ability. On the contrary, Originals are normal people who have tried a lot and failed a lot. Originals test out many ideas, discard the mountains of bad ones, and keep the few good ideas. Putting yourself out there when the outcome is uncertain can be a scary thing. Putting yourself out there after failing time and time again is even scarier. Originals manage this fear of failure through expression of idea doubt. Idea doubt is questioning whether an idea is good enough or not. When faced with idea doubt, Originals find ways to test and refine their ideas, ultimately increasing their probability of success. Idea doubt's evil twin is self-doubt. Self-doubt is questioning whether we are good enough. Instead of analyzing the aspects of the idea, we internalize the problem and question our self-worth. We see a bad idea that failed as a reflection of ourselves as a failure. While idea doubt can be motivating, self-doubt can be paralyzing and can prevent us from moving in any direction.[56]

If you are a woman or person of color, you may be highly susceptible to the self-doubt trap. Added up, the negative stereotypes associated with your identity, the assumptions made about your abilities, and the pressures you face in a work setting can be crippling. Concern about making a mistake can prevent you from ever taking a risk. If you are happy with where you are, then it is OK to take the safe route. However, if you are hoping to move to the next level, you will need to take some calculated risks.

Taking a risk requires self-confidence and assertiveness, two areas in which women and professionals of color often struggle. The book *The Confidence Code*, written by Katty Kay and Claire Shipman, posits that there is a significant confidence gap between the genders. Women are generally less confident and less assertive than men, even when they have equal or greater qualifications.[57] Confidence and assertiveness are particularly challenging for women because of the societal/cultural expectations placed on us to be humble and demure. Women at all levels, even at the tops of their fields, need to constantly assert and reassert themselves.

After one of my presentations on this topic of acting like a winner, a young woman shared a story with me that brought this point to life. Jasmine, a Black woman, was trying to decide between two job offers. Her top job choice was in a field she was highly qualified for and deeply passionate about. The only downside was that the salary offer was much lower than she had hoped. Her second choice was in a field that was still interesting to her and would provide some learning opportunities and a higher salary. That is what she was telling herself, anyway, because of the significantly higher salary that came with the job. Tired of going back and forth on her decision, she called her friend Rachel, a White woman, for advice. When Jasmine explained her situation, Rachel told her to follow her passions and the money would figure itself out (i.e., take the lower-paying job). The thing that mattered the most at the end of the day was whether or not you truly loved your job.

While Jasmine was thinking over Rachel's words, she heard a voice in the background saying, "That's terrible advice. Give me the phone right now." Suddenly, Rachel's husband, Steve, was on the line. He apologized because he normally did not like to get involved in his wife's personal conversations. However, he had made an exception in this case because he couldn't stand the bad advice his wife was giving to one of their good friends. Steve told Jasmine to go back to her top-choice company, clearly lay out the value she would bring to the job, and demand a higher salary. Jasmine mentioned the company had said this was a final, nonnegotiable offer. Steve insisted that if Jasmine acted like a winner and showed the company that she knew her value, the company would come back with a better offer.

Going against the voice in her head, Jasmine followed Steve's advice, and lo and behold, the company agreed to the higher salary request. Jasmine had both her dream job and her dream salary. All she had had to do was "act like a man" during the negotiation to get them. Jasmine called Rachel back after receiving the offer and told her, "Steve was right! All I had to do was channel my inner White male."

EXECUTIVE PRESENCE: GRAVITAS, COMMUNICATION, APPEARANCE

Another way to think about adopting the mindset of a winner in your professional life is exhibiting executive presence. Sylvia Ann Hewlett, an economist and researcher on gender and workplace issues, identified three components of executive presence: gravitas, communication, and appearance. *Gravitas* refers to the way you carry yourself, *communication* is all about how you articulate ideas, and *appearance* entails looking the part. Although they are interdependent, they are not weighted equally. When 268 senior executives were asked which component was most important for executive presence, 67 percent said gravitas, 28 percent said communication, and 5 percent said professional appearance. Gravitas was by far the most important component and, incidentally, the hardest to define. When asked to define *gravitas*, the senior executives surveyed most commonly said "the ability to maintain composure in stressful situations."[58]

DEMONSTRATE GRAVITAS THROUGH NON-VERBAL COMMUNICATION

Gravitas, or the aura of leadership, can come across through your nonverbal communication. Nonverbal communication refers to your body language. The way you position your body conveys something to the other people in the room. In turn, we make judgments based on other people's body language. We may not realize it, but we can communicate a lot even when we don't utter a single word. Nonverbal communication can have a significant impact on a variety of outcomes in our lives, from whether or not we get hired to whether or not we can successfully command the room.

DEVELOP YOUR VERBAL COMMUNICATION

Your calm demeanor under pressure alone will not secure you a top spot at your organization. Another important component is the ability to communicate your ideas confidently and clearly. This is a difficult task, especially for women who are often interrupted and talked over. A 2017 study analyzing Supreme Court oral arguments conducted by a Northwestern University law professor found that male justices interrupt female justices far more often than the other way around. Furthermore, male lawyers interrupt female justices more often than they do male justices. When all is said and done, female justices speak less frequently and say fewer words than male justices.[59] These findings highlight a theme that is present in many organizations—men speak over women, and men interrupt women. This happens even on the Supreme Court and even when there is a distinct difference in status (lawyer to justice). Women need to be conscious of this practice and try to actively disrupt it. Men need to be conscious of this practice and try to disrupt it as well—before a woman calls them out on it and says they have unconscious bias based on gender.

Below are a few strategies for communicating your thoughts clearly and succinctly.

OPERATIONAL STRATEGIES: EFFECTIVE COMMUNICATION[60]

- Golden Rule: say what you mean and mean what you say.
- Get to the point. Don't dilute and obscure your message with a long preamble or unnecessary details. Whenever possible, try to make your point using half as many words.

- Become well versed in the lingo used in your field. Read the news and industry-relevant publications to stay informed and contribute when conversations arise.

The last component of executive presence is professional appearance. We will cover this topic in depth in "Rule 6: Invest in Your Professional Appearance."

BE OPEN TO CONSTRUCTIVE FEEDBACK

One of the most important keys to developing executive presence is receiving direct, honest feedback from trusted sources around you. Not many people will give you the unsolicited, constructive criticism you need to hear. Let's be clear here. There is a difference between criticism and constructive criticism. It is up to you to identify the difference when it comes your way. As an aspiring professional with a growth mindset, you should demonstrate that you won't avoid or ignore constructive criticism.

Getting feedback is vital to your success. If you react poorly to constructive feedback, then you are less likely to receive it from those around you. And don't make the mistake of thinking you are perfect just because you haven't received constructive criticism in a while. It is more likely that your colleagues and bosses, even your friends and family, are holding back instead of thinking that you are flawless. With trusted sources, there is no shame in asking for an honest appraisal of your strengths and weaknesses. After receiving feedback, it is important to process the advice and implement change. This is easier said than done. Sometimes the feedback we get is contradictory. This is especially troublesome for women, who are given messages like be feminine but not too feminine and assertive but not too assertive. An astonishing 81 percent of women who receive feedback report difficulty understanding it and translating it into action.[61]

Below are a few operational strategies for how to react to criticism when it comes your way.

OPERATIONAL STRATEGIES: RECEIVING CRITICISM

- Resist the urge to be defensive. If you have a dismissive facial expression or immediately try to explain your actions, then the other person may shut down and stop giving you feedback.
- Ask clarifying questions. Sometimes in order to protect our egos, we don't engage fully in a discussion when someone is criticizing us. Make sure that you completely understand the feedback you are being given.
- Ask for concrete examples of abstract feedback. Having specific examples in mind gives us a tangible starting point for addressing the feedback. It also helps confirm that this criticism is based on facts as opposed to something else.
- Categorize the feedback as constructive or not. Be honest in your assessment. If the feedback was constructive, determine the best way to follow up. Depending on the situation, it may be best to request a follow-up meeting after you have had some time to fully process the feedback.

CONCLUSION

The reason I address the psychological game is because most diverse professionals are either underprepared for the long road ahead or disillusioned about their odds of success and quit early. A significant portion of professionals of color don't see a clear path to the top. According to research produced by the Center for Talent Innovation (CTI), 21 percent of Hispanics, 29 percent of Asians, and 35 percent of Black/African Americans don't think a person of color will ever reach a top leadership position at their organization. The professionals who responded this way likely know the bias and discrimination that exists in their workplaces. What options do these professionals have? Most people suggest that they voice their concerns and engage in a respectful dialogue about their feelings. In my experience, that has rarely been a useful course of action. CTI research shows that more than a third of Asians and Hispanics and half of all Black/African Americans felt they would face negative repercussions if they ever tried to report bias or discrimination in the office. So, when faced with bias and discrimination, professionals put on a mask when they enter the workplace. An alarming 37 percent of Black/African Americans and Hispanics and 45 percent of Asians report that they can't be their authentic selves at work. These professionals may have adopted the mentality that, since the culture has always been this way, it is easier to try to fit in than to speak up against it.[62]

It is important to recognize that the issue of bringing your authentic self to the workplace affects people who feel marginalized based on some aspect of their identity. When we feel unwelcomed or uncomfortable due to individuals being oblivious to the effects of their actions, we are not always in the mood to educate them. One thing is for certain: no matter what happens, you always need to remember that you are a value-added player. No one can take that away from you. You are a valuable addition to any team and a prized asset for any potential employer. Never forget your self-worth. The road ahead is long, and the odds may be challenging, but achieving your vision is definitely possible. With the right mindset and accompanying actions, you can achieve anything you set your mind to. Start with a strong psychological foundation, and you will be more resilient on the path toward your dream.

Rule 3

THE NUMBERS MATTER

Identify and prioritize all the metrics that matter.

There is nothing quite so useless as doing with great efficiency something that should not be done at all.

—PETER DRUCKER

In "Rule 1: Success Is Intentional," we discussed the importance of coming up with a personal definition of success. For example, you may have set a goal of getting promoted to the next level. This section will address how your organization views your performance. Once you know the metrics on which you are being evaluated, you can focus on developing those aspects of your game—namely, the ones that really matter.

IDENTIFY YOUR ORGANIZATION'S PRIORITIES

All organizations have goals. The executive leadership typically sets the priorities for each year based on the organization's short-term and long-term goals. Information gets filtered as it is passed through the ranks on a need-to-know basis. If you want to advance in your workplace, you need to have a good grasp of how your work fits into the bigger picture.

In most cases, the primary objectives are easily identifiable. You may be able to identify these goals through the organization's mission statement and published annual reports and during your performance review. For-profit entities are generally concerned about their profitability. These companies want to know how your efforts affect their bottom lines. During your performance review, you may be asked, directly or indirectly, to talk about how your efforts either significantly boosted revenues or cut costs to make the organization more profitable. However, your performance review is rarely one dimensional. Your contribution to the company's bottom line may be just one of many criteria on which you are evaluated. Although it may require some effort asking around, you need to identify *all* the priorities of your organization. When starting a new job or executing a plan to get promoted, finding out the exact criteria that matter to your organization shows initiative, but it will also ensure that you are focusing on the right things. By having a clear understanding of what matters to your organization, you can focus your energy in the right places.

TWO REASONS IDENTIFYING PRIORITIES IS HARD

Organizations have a list of objectives and metrics that are used to measure whether individuals are accomplishing the organization's priorities. Your organization is no different. Make sure you are focusing on the firm's priorities and not exclusively your own. Strive for a win-win situation. Find ways to add value to your company while also setting yourself up to achieve your goals. In many cases, however, it is not always clear on what metrics you are being evaluated.

One of the reasons I joined the U.S. Attorney's Office was to get trial experience for my goal of being a trial lawyer. In my first year there, my main focus was going to trial. What I didn't realize until after my first performance review was that trials and trial performance were not key metrics for getting an outstanding performance review. What I learned during my performance review was that it mattered how many cases you filed and defendants you indicted, key metrics for the office's performance, and that you cleared your docket of cases that could never be prosecuted or that you had decided not to prosecute. So all my trials really didn't earn me an outstanding rating that first year. In the second year, I had a better understanding, and I achieved the metrics that mattered for the U.S. Attorney's Office as well as trying cases, something that mattered to me. That's an example of a win-win approach.

There are two main reasons why the metrics aren't always clear to you.

1. Hidden Metrics

    As demonstrated above, some of the metrics you are evaluated on are not always intuitive. What matters to the organization may seem trivial to you and vice versa. It is important to align your efforts with the organization's priorities to set yourself up for advancement.

2. Changing Metrics

    Second, the metrics that matter change over time as you climb the ladder. Each year, you must recalibrate the measuring stick to determine if and how the evaluation criteria for job performance have changed. In a law firm, associates are often evaluated based on the quantity of billable hours and the quality of their work. While billable hours still matter at the partner level, business development is an added crucial component of success at this higher level. To continue your rise to the top, it is important to be receptive to information about what matters to the organization at your level.

FINDING OUT WHAT MATTERS

There are always numbers that matter with respect to your performance in professional services organizations. Both the quality and the quantity of work matters. Quality means high-profile (i.e., for important clients) or high-impact matters on which you do an excellent job. Quantity means the hours billed. Make sure you are on target for at least the minimum number of hours and, to the extent that you can determine the median, you would be well served to be in the upper 50 percent with respect to hours. If you are a partner, it is likely that business origination and realization matters as well as the number of hours. Determine whether your contribution to increasing the business that an institutional client gives the firm provides any benefit to your career. You will know by how it is measured and whether there are any monetary benefits associated with it. If committee participation matters within your firm, make sure you have a significant role on a committee where participation is valued, such as Hiring or the Diversity Committee—or even better the Management or Compensation Committee. The bottom line is you need to discern the priorities and make sure you are putting your maximum effort in the areas that matter to your firm. If you decide to stray from these priorities, at least do so intentionally, recognizing that it is likely to affect your ultimate success at the firm—either in the short term, the long term, or both.

HITTING YOUR NUMBERS

In the professional services context, the number of hours billed is a proxy for the level of experience in the organization. If your company has a goal of 2,400 hours per year and you only bill 1,200 hours, then you are only considered half as experienced as your peer who billed 2,400 hours. It is not only important to hit your goal for the year, but also the composition of your work hours matters. Client-related work is always seen as more valuable than non-billable work (e.g., articles, training, *pro bono*). In senior positions at professional services firms, such as law, accounting, and consulting firms, business development matters as well. Business development is about how much revenue you bring into your firm and matters much more as you get into more senior levels.

Another important point to note is that most departments have a budget. If you are responsible for the department budget or a piece of it, stay within it. Exceeding your budget without express authorization is a major problem in both for-profit and not-for-profit organizations. That applies to both a time budget (hours billed) and a financial budget. In addition to the numbers, reliability and timeliness matter much more than you think. Failing to honor deadlines makes you unreliable. Being deemed unreliable will hamper your promotion possibilities and access to great work. As you move up, you need to understand which metrics are factored into advancement/promotion decisions.

BE RELIABLY ERROR FREE

Work with errors, even minor ones, makes you unreliable. If you produce work with errors, someone else will have to go back and fix your mistakes. The cause of every mistake can be attributed either to the person (fixed state) or to the situation (flexible state). Fundamental attribution error describes the tendency that people have to overestimate internal factors (personality and disposition) and underestimate external factors (circumstances of the situation) when explaining someone's behavior.[63] When you make a small mistake, fundamental attribution error tells us that people are more likely to consider that mistake a result of your lack of intelligence than a one-off misstep related to the situation.

Minor errors matter even more for diverse people because of unconscious bias and stereotypes that people tend to have about these groups. For example, let's take a look at how stereotypes factor in when an individual commits a small math error. There are no widely accepted negative stereotypes about White men's math ability. Therefore, if you are a White male, a small math error may just be seen as the result of you having an off day. This flexibility is less likely to be given to women and minorities. Women, Black/African Americans, and Hispanics are stereotypically considered to be bad at math. If you are a part of one of these diverse groups and you make a math error, it is likely to be given more weight. A supervisor may think that the negative stereotype about you is confirmed and may avoid giving you important quantitative tasks in the future. Asians are considered to be stereotypically good at math. If you are Asian and make a minor math mistake, people may think you must be having a bad day. You will most likely be given another chance to prove yourself.

Moving beyond quantitative skills, verbal skills are also incredibly important. Therefore, spelling and grammar errors also matter. It is not a big leap for your boss to think that if you make errors on the little things, you will also make errors on the big things. These little mistakes contribute significantly to how people in the office view your work and may prevent you from receiving important projects in the future. You should also be aware that managers often talk about your work. Therefore, one error may become known to other managers.

The following are a few operational strategies for reducing the number of errors in your work.

OPERATIONAL STRATEGIES: REDUCING ERRORS

- Read e-mails and other written content out loud. You are likely to catch awkward phrasing and grammatical errors when you hear a sentence as opposed to simply reading it.
- Double- and triple-check your work, especially in the early stages of forming a working relationship with a coworker. When there is not a long-established working relationship, the other

members of your team are forming their impressions of your capabilities and reliability from your early work product.

- If you make a mistake, correct it as soon as possible without calling more attention than required to the situation. It is better for you to catch your own mistake than for someone else to point it out to you. Identify how the error happened and make sure the same error doesn't happen again.

- Make sure you understand the assignment. Check in informally in order to "course correct" before the final product is due and evaluated.

BEYOND THE METRICS: THE SUBJECTIVE COMPONENT

Although your company will keep track of your numbers throughout the year, you may only talk about them once a year at your annual performance evaluation. If you are lucky, maybe you meet with a supervisor/manager a few times a year to discuss your progress. These employee performance evaluations are important because they are used to determine bonuses, pay raises, and promotions. These performance evaluations comprise objective and subjective components. We have already touched on the objective components. These are the metrics that matter to your company. It is important to always meet or exceed your targets so you are near the top of the pack when it comes time for bonuses, raises, and promotions.

At the same time, it is important not to discount subjective performance measures. Objective measures are not always available or robust, so they are often supplemented with subjective measures. Research shows that a relationship exists between subjective performance ratings and an employee's career progression. More specifically, the study found that subjective performance ratings were correlated with base pay, bonuses, promotions, demotions, and dismissals.[64]

Intuitively, this makes sense. For example, if two people who are up for promotion bill the same number of hours, it can be helpful to have a supervisor's opinion on what their performance was like beyond what the numbers demonstrate. The problematic aspect of a subjective evaluation is that it can be influenced by unconscious bias. Since the dominant group shapes the workplace culture, unconscious bias disproportionately affects minority groups negatively. People with disabilities, people who are LGBT, racial and ethnic minorities, and women may all find themselves in the minority group at their organization and experiencing unconscious bias.

To see an example of how subjective evaluations affect outcomes, take a look at the following chart, which highlights some comments made about male and female entrepreneurs who were seeking funding from government venture capitalists.[65]

Comparing How Male and Female Entrepreneurs Are Described by Venture Capitalists

These gendered personas are illustrated with quotes from Swedish government VCs who were observed discussing a total of 125 applications for funding between 2009 and 2010.

The average MALE entrepreneur is described with attributes such as:	The average FEMALE entrepreneur is described with attributes such as:
■ "Young and promising"	■ "Young, but inexperienced"
■ "Arrogant, but very impressive competence"	■ "Lacks network contacts and in need of help to develop her business concept"
■ "Aggressive, but a really good entrepreneur"	■ "Enthusiastic, but weak"
■ "Experienced and knowledgeable"	■ "Experienced, but worried"
■ "Very competent innovator and already has money to play with"	■ "Good-looking and careless with money"
■ "Cautious, sensible, and level-headed"	■ "Too cautious and does not dare"
■ "Extremely capable and very driven"	■ "Lacks ability for venturing and growth"
■ "Educated engineer at a prestigious university and has run businesses before"	■ "Visionary, but with no knowledge of the market"

NOTE QUOTES WERE TRANSLATED FROM SWEDISH TO ENGLISH.
SOURCE "GENDER STEREOTYPES AND VENTURE SUPPORT DECISIONS: HOW GOVERNMENTAL VENTURE CAPITALISTS SOCIALLY CONSTRUCT ENTREPRENEURS' POTENTIAL," BY MALIN MALMSTRÖM ET AL., ENTREPRENEURSHIP THEORY AND PRACTICE, FEBRUARY 2017

© HBR.ORG

Based on these comments, which group do you think was less likely to get funding? The female entrepreneurs. Applications were dismissed for around 53 percent of females compared to 38 percent of males. Even when granted funding, women received on average just 25 percent of their desired amount. Men, however, received on average 52 percent of their desired amount.[66] This example underscores the importance of paying attention to subjective evaluations about your ability.

In the rules of the game that follow, we will walk through some strategies to combat unconscious bias and make a positive impression in the workplace. Because subjective evaluations vary greatly, one of the best ways to get known for the right reasons is to exceed the expectations set for you on quantifiable metrics. It is your job to figure out what numbers matter in your company with respect to your performance and deliver in those areas.

Below is a set of strategies for fully understanding your performance review to identify how your organization sees your value.

OPERATIONAL STRATEGIES: UNDERSTANDING THE METRICS

- Acquire a copy of your company's performance evaluation form, ideally when you begin your job, so you can see all the items that feed into your overall score.
- Ask your mentors, supervisors, trusted peers, and HR what types of experiences are valued in each category.
- Get your completed review "translated" by a mentor or veteran who works at the company. If you are new to the company, it may be hard to gauge if your performance review went well. To make sure you understand how the organization truly views you, you should ask your mentor to translate the potentially coded language that may show up in your performance review.

- Throughout the year, fill out your performance appraisal form based on the projects and initiatives you complete. Aim to have two to three concrete examples for each category. Catalogue how your successes and accomplishments fulfill the organization's goals. Then when it's time to write your self-evaluation, you will have plenty of examples to share. (Don't rely on your or your manager's memory.)

HOW YOU STACK UP COMPARED TO YOUR PEERS

All comparisons are relative. You not only need to perform well, but you also need to be near the top of your peer group to make it to the next level. Sometimes it can be difficult to know where you stand in relation to your peers. Please don't become ultracompetitive and devise ways to sabotage your peers. You should always aim to elevate your game rather than to push others down. Just knowing where you land among those in your position can be helpful. During your performance review, ask explicitly where you fall among your cohort.

If you can't get the information regarding your comparative performance from your supervisors, there are other ways of finding out how much your company values you. Two key data points are salary and bonuses. Organizations are often reluctant to share salary and bonus information. One way to get around this is to form an information-sharing group with your peers. I have worked in places where the peers in a cohort anonymously share their raise percentages and bonuses in order to understand how they rank compared to their peers. One person collects the information and captures it for all to see. This type of information exchange can be beneficial for all involved.

When I worked at a law firm, I had no way of knowing if the firm thought I was doing a good job or not. I got a bonus at the end of every year, but so did everybody else. A group of my peers wanted to know how everyone ranked among the class but still wanted to maintain privacy. We came up with the following system. After we received our year-end bonuses, we would all get together to exchange information. We found that the best way to share was for everyone to write down his or her bonus amount on a piece of paper and put it in a hat. Then one person would take all the pieces of paper out one by one and create a ranked list of everyone's bonuses. The dollar amounts were not associated with employee names. When the list was shown, you knew what your number was and could easily see where you stood in relation to your peers. You, too, can set this up informally within your network if your company fails to provide this information.

The following are a couple of operational strategies for determining your relevant standing in the organization vis-à-vis your peers.

OPERATIONAL STRATEGIES: PEER COMPARISON

- Figure out how you compare to your peers. Either ask during your performance review or find an outlet to discreetly and anonymously share information within your cohort.
- Understand how the expectations of your position change over time as you become more senior in your organization. With each promotion, your peer group changes, and the metrics change. Keep up to date on the changes and step up your game accordingly.

CONCLUSION

Time is a scarce resource. We are all given 24 hours in a day. Between sleeping, eating, and commuting, we use up around 10 to 12 hours. Even if we spent every waking moment working, we could not keep up with the ever-growing list of possible to-dos. Therefore, it is important for us to focus our time and energy on the areas that have the most impact on the outcomes that are important to us. Knowing the metrics that matter in your career will allow you to work smarter by investing your limited time and energy into the areas that matter for your performance evaluations and, ultimately, for your success in your current role.

Rule 4

ACTIVELY NETWORK

Building relationships is essential to long-term success.

*If you want to go fast, go alone. If you
want to go far, go together.*

—*AFRICAN PROVERB*

You show up to work well rested and ready to hit the ground running. You grab a cup of coffee (or your drink of choice) and head straight to your office to make a plan for the day. You settle in at your desk, silently nod to your office mate, and close the door so you can focus better with fewer distractions. You sit down at your desk and plan out what you need to accomplish that day. When you look at your list, you realize you have quite a lot to do. You tell yourself that if you power through the day, you can complete your ambitious to-do list. Remembering the lesson from the book *The 7 Habits of Highly Effective People*, you "eat your frog first" (start with the day's hardest task) and work your way through your list.[67]

An acquaintance or two swing by your office and ask if you want to grab lunch. You respond that you have a busy day and will try to catch up with them later. After your office friends leave, you glance at the clock and realize it is around lunchtime. You had been so focused on your work that you lost track of time. Since you are in the middle of a task, you decide to do a working lunch. You grab some food and have lunch while continuing to chip away at your pile of work.

Your office mate starts packing up for the day and asks if you plan to attend the company's happy hour. You are nearing the end of your to-do list and decide to forego the work social to stay a little later to finish up your work. When you finally emerge from your desk, you realize most of the people in the office are gone. Since it is dinnertime, you head home for food and sleep. You know you will most likely have another busy day tomorrow. You tell yourself to take things one day at a time. If you continue to work hard, then you will move up the ladder at work. Plus, that's the advice your parents have always given you—work hard, and you will go far.

Many of you can probably relate to the scenario above. It may be an experience you have had a few times. For others, it may be your day-to-day experience at work. You consider yourself a hard worker who produces high-quality work and will often work through lunch with hopes that your hard work will be noticed and rewarded with a promotion or the best projects. Contrary to what you might think, simply sitting at your desk and doing all your work isn't enough to move up in the workplace—especially to move up past the midlevel. Exceeding expectations and doing high-quality work keep you in the game, but they're not the key to moving to a leadership position.

The truth is, there is no single key to advancing to a leadership position. Over the next few chapters, we will discuss the importance of networking, finding mentors and sponsors, investing in your professional appearance, self-promoting, and establishing yourself as a key player. These unwritten rules all play a role in your career success. The rule of the game that we will focus on in this chapter is networking. Networking is the art of building, nurturing, and utilizing relationships. Taking time to cultivate strong relationships can help you create a safety net to catch you when you are down and open up doors you never knew existed to reach greater heights. Your network is also a source of your power in the world. Your network can expand your influence in the world. You can access it to make things happen for yourself, for others, and for causes you care about. At least three relationship-building opportunities were missed in the scenario above. Did you catch all three?

1. The worker could have spent a few minutes engaging in small talk with his or her office mate before making a plan for the day. Instead, with a simple acknowledgment of the office mate's existence, the worker dove headfirst into the pile of work.

2. The worker had the opportunity to catch up with an office friend over lunch. Everyone has to eat, and meals are a great way to strengthen a relationship. On an especially busy day, the worker could have at least walked with the friend to pick up lunch before heading back to his or her desk. The elevator ride, the walk to the local food court, and the wait in line are all prime times for a mini check-in with work friends. This also fosters the informal exchange of workplace information.

3. The worker would have been well served by making an appearance, even a brief one, at the company's happy hour. Company social events are set up for you not only to strengthen bonds with office friends but also to get to know colleagues you may not have interacted with before. Meeting people in other departments might give you insight into job opportunities or open positions you otherwise might not have heard about. You might miss opportunities to form informal mentoring relationships. By forgoing the event and working late in hopes of getting recognized,

the worker is more likely to fall further into obscurity as few people in the company know or remember him or her.

NETWORKING

To be frank, many people think of networking as unpleasant or exploitative. Some people believe in being independent and earning their successes through hard work. While these are noble notions, overreliance on doing everything ourselves can stall our careers as we see those around us move on to better things.

A professor at Stanford University Graduate School of Business conducted a study to discover what traits the most successful MBA alumni had in common. The professor wanted to see if grade point average, standardized test scores, or personality traits could be used as predictors of success. For a group of MBA alumni, these three data points were recorded along with their compensation 5, 10, 15, and 20 years after graduation. The study revealed that the only variable that was a positive predictor of financial success throughout the MBAs' careers was a personality trait: social extroversion.[68] This finding highlights the link between the ability to make social connections and career success. A robust network can help you achieve your career goals. Networking is, at its core, based on developing relationships with people you like and helping one another in a reciprocal manner. Knowing people who are willing to help you and who have information you may need can be useful to you (or your friends or clients) professionally and personally. You have probably heard that the world operates on a relationship basis. This is especially true in business. It matters who you know, who trusts you, and who owes you a favor. The strongest professional relationships comprise individuals who are willing to do favors for one another when asked. When tapping into your professional network to complete an objective, make sure you follow the rule of reciprocity. You need to be willing to do someone else a favor because you are going to be asking him or her for a favor. The person with the most extensive network of people who hold him or her in high regard and who can access that network when needed is ultimately the most successful.

HOW TO BUILD YOUR NETWORK

You cannot build the type of network you need to be successful by sitting at your desk and working all the time. You can meet individuals through a variety of different activities in which you may be engaged. You can build relationships with people at work, especially if your office has affinity groups, employee resource groups, or sports teams. You can build relationships with people when you are involved in civic or not-for-profit activities. You can build relationships in professional or alumni associations or with the parents of your children's friends. You can build relationships participating in religious activities or sports teams.

In the networking guide *Never Eat Alone,* the author outlines a few faulty mindsets that you should avoid so you can make the most of your networking opportunities. Don't be a "Wallflower," taking on the role of silent spectator and avoiding conversations with other people at an event. Don't be an "Ankle Hugger," clinging on to the first person you meet out of fear that you will be alone during a networking event. And don't be a "Celebrity Hound," pursuing a big-name contact and ignoring all the lesser-known people who could be tremendously valuable contacts as well.[69] Ultimately, the key is to adopt the mindset that anyone you meet could potentially become a valuable part of your network.

After making the initial connection, you need to nurture relationships with people in your network by e-mailing them, calling them, and meeting them for lunch. You can nurture your network by working in charitable activities, civic activities, bar association activities, or business activities with them. How you stay connected to different members of your network can vary greatly, but one thing is constant—you must stay in touch. Good follow-up can help you stand apart from your peers because most people either don't follow up or are bad at it. Ideally, you should follow up within 24 hours after meeting a new contact and program your calendar to send you a reminder to touch base with the contact a month later. Timely follow-ups can ensure that you remember your contact and that your contact remembers you.[70]

Below is a list of operational strategies aimed to help you better connect with new and old contacts in your network.

OPERATIONAL STRATEGIES: STAYING IN TOUCH

- Strive to form a meaningful connection. Don't measure your networking success by how many business cards you give away or collect. If the contact doesn't remember you or value the connection and vice versa, then it is ultimately useless.
- Include a personal touch that demonstrates thoughtfulness in each message. Sending mass e-mails and generic cards are not effective at nurturing business relationships.
- Follow-up messages should be concise and sent in a timely manner. In your follow-up message, include a memorable portion of the conversation you had or the context in which you met and any commitments you made to each other.
- If applicable, send a note to the person who put you in touch with a new contact, thanking him or her for the effort.
- Whenever possible, use mealtimes as mini breaks to catch up with an office friend or develop a relationship with a new contact. People love to bond over food.
- Host a dinner party or brunch over the weekend. It is a great way to maximize your time and catch up with many people in the same place. It also allows the opportunity for people in your network to get to know one another.

THE VALUE OF A DIVERSE NETWORK

You want to be very strategic in terms of how you build your network. Your network needs to be as diverse as the world in which you live. To be most effective, you need to network across racial, sexual orientation, and gender lines, among other lines of difference. There is an active old-boy network and an old-girl network, and the diverse professionals network is growing and getting stronger as well. You need to be able to access all these networks when it is appropriate.

Additionally, you will find that being recognized as an external player will provide you with more value within the firm or company. Clients will seek you out for access to your network, and so will your colleagues. You can get things done when others cannot. You have increased your value and your opportunities by nurturing and developing your network. The reach of your network could span various industries and include people in all types of positions. By maintaining positive relationships with all people, you will be more successful. You should treat office administrative staff as well as professionals and your peers with respect. The administrative staff can be great sources of information. While CEOs, vice presidents, and partners of organizations make high-level strategic decisions, their administrative staffs are tasked with delivering the information to the appropriate parties. Assistants are also gatekeepers for their bosses' schedules. If you want to schedule a meeting with an individual at the top of an organization, it doesn't hurt to know the assistant making the schedule. If you always treat the administrative staff with dignity and acknowledge their help, then the doors to even the most powerful decision-makers may open for you.

As a senior lawyer working for a corporation, I often needed to get the CEO's approval on a litigation settlement. Time was usually short to obtain the approval. Staying on good terms with the CEO's executive assistant meant she would work hard to squeeze me into a packed schedule. I am certain that others who were disrespectful to her were just told to wait a month or so for the next available appointment.

Below is a list of operational strategies for how to build a strong network.

OPERATIONAL STRATEGIES: BUILDING YOUR NETWORK

- Network across racial, ethnic, sexual orientation, and gender lines, among others.
- Develop relationships with "go-to" people long before you need to ask for a favor.
- Treat office administrative staff and your peers with respect.
- Be nice to everyone, including secretaries and assistants. Often ignored, these individuals control the flow of information to their bosses, oversee the scheduling of meetings, and can provide you important information and access.
- If you don't enjoy company networking functions, go early and let as many people see you as possible. I call it "see and be seen." Then you can leave when it is crowded, and no one will know when you left. They will only remember that you were there.
- Be willing to sit with the boss. Many leaders say people often avoid them at events. Don't do that. They will remember you favorably.

BREADTH VS. DEPTH OF CONNECTIONS

When you think about building relationships, there are two factors that you need to balance: breadth and depth. *Breadth* refers to how many people are in your network. *Depth* refers to the meaningfulness of each relationship. On one extreme, you could have an expansive network of superficial connections. At the other extreme, you could have a very close relationship with just one or two people. Typically, deep relationships are more personally satisfying in the present moment and are more likely to involve a positive favor exchange in the future. As you grow your network, remember the age-old adage: quality over quantity. With technology, we have developed larger social networks held together by weaker bonds. We have on average 200 social media friends, 11 offline friends, and 5 close friends. For the most intimate friendships, the ones in which we discuss our most private information, we typically only have 2 people to call on.[71] As you meet more and more people over the course of your life, you will be faced with decisions about which relationships to nurture and which to let go. When you are in that position, let go of the shallow relationships that aren't fulfilling to you, either personally or professionally. There is no use having a long list of contacts if you do not feel comfortable reaching out to half of them when you need something.

It is vital to note the difference between your personal network and your professional network. All your business contacts comprise your professional network. All your family and friends comprise your personal network. You access these two networks for different reasons, so it is important to keep them separate. Your personal network should serve as an endless source of emotional support, where no one is keeping score. Your professional network can also be accessed as a source of support for your goals, but your favor is granted with the expectation of being repaid in kind. Plus, you shouldn't share private information with people in your professional network. For example, most of us have some distant family members who may make poor choices. You don't need to share that your cousin has a drug problem or was arrested last weekend. Some aspects of your personal life should remain private at work.

The following are a couple of operational strategies for how to focus on quality contacts so your network feels meaningful to you.

OPERATIONAL STRATEGIES: THOUGHTFULLY MAKING CONNECTIONS

- Do your research and look up the people you want to meet at an event. It is much easier to have an engaging conversation when you are not starting from scratch.
- Develop a network of friends and family as a source of support for personal matters. Keep this support network separate from your professional network. Make sure you nurture it by spending time with this valuable network.

MAINTAIN A POSITIVE IMAGE

In your organization, you want to establish yourself as a leader or "go-to" person to whom people want to be connected. For this to be the case, you have to work to distinguish yourself from your peers. One of the best ways to distinguish yourself from your peers is to be a "can-do" person as opposed to someone who often says no. Clients seek out professionals who can help them achieve their goals. Your client may want to achieve his or her goal by taking a path that is unwise or possibly illegal. It is your job not only to explain why the client's path is inadvisable, but also to come up with an alternative plan to help your client achieve his or her goal within the law.

If you find a way to reliably deliver results, especially in difficult situations, people will begin to view you as a "go-to" person. When you build a strong reputation at your office, people will want to work with you and will want to be in your network. As you build your reputation as a "go-to" person, identify and connect with the other "go-to" people in your office. Be mindful of the people you are connecting to in your network. For better or worse, the reputation and perception of the people in your network will rub off on you. You have probably heard the expression "Birds of a feather flock together." It is true. As I said before, you cannot soar like an eagle if you hang around with pigeons.

CLIENT/BUSINESS DEVELOPMENT

For people who have responsibility in the area of client development, also known as business development or rainmaking, having relationships is key to being able to successfully develop business and sell their or their firm's services. And you should know that making rain requires substantial effort on your part. Business development is particularly important in professional services firms. Begin building relationships that may lead to client or business development early. That means when you first start out in your career, you want to get to know as many people as possible. You never know where your contacts will end up in 5, 10, or 15 years. Being on good terms with them now may benefit you later. It is never too early to start. College and graduate school relationships and alumni networks can be very important to future success.

Many people know the benefits of a strong network. Because of the reciprocal nature of the relationship, people who are connected trade favors.

UTILIZING YOUR NETWORK: ASKING FOR FAVORS

Knowing everyone doesn't necessarily get you anywhere, unless those people are willing to step up when you need a favor. People may do a favor for you out of the kindness of their hearts or, more commonly, because you have done or will do a favor for them. It is the favor exchange that ends up deepening the relationship and strengthening your network. Not all relationships need to involve favors being exchanged. But typically, that is the nature of relationships. In your personal relationships, you are constantly doing things for people close to you, and they are constantly doing things for you. It is just that you don't think about it as an exchange, *per se.*

In your professional life, you should keep a mental balance sheet of the favors you have done and the favors you have cashed in. Favors are not easily quantifiable, but you should make note of and try to balance the amount of effort required to complete the favors in a favor exchange. When you ask someone to do something for you, offer to help them out in return. If they don't ask for anything in the moment, then be open to doing them a favor at some point in the future. Many favors are exchanged at different points in time. You can offer unsolicited favors to people in your professional network to build up a favor bank to cash in at a later date when the need arises.

Below are a few operational strategies for developing the proper mindset regarding the exchange of favors that occurs in your network interactions. Effectively utilizing your network can have numerous benefits, a few of which are discussed below.

OPERATIONAL STRATEGIES: ASKING FOR FAVORS

- Whenever you request a favor, ask what you can do in return.
- Keep a mental account of favors received and favors granted, but don't keep a strict score.
- Be willing to give generously within your means. You will reap the rewards in due time.

BENEFIT #1: FINDING A JOB

A classic 1974 study titled *Getting a Job* gives some credence to the saying "It's not what you know but who you know that matters." In the study, a group of men in Newton, Massachusetts, were asked how they got their current jobs. Of all respondents, around 10 percent had applied directly to an employer. The majority of respondents (56 percent) leveraged personal connections to get their jobs. Interestingly enough, these personal connections were more often acquaintances than close friends. Of the people who leveraged personal connections to get their jobs, 55 percent met their contacts only occasionally, and 28 percent rarely interacted with their contacts. Why is it that these individuals benefited from reaching out to someone they spoke to infrequently? One explanation is that acquaintances, also known as "weak ties," operated in different circles than the job seekers. By reaching out to them, the individuals were able to get access to new people and new information outside their immediate circle, both of which are helpful during a job search. Therefore, it is important to be on good terms with all the people in your network, no matter how frequently you see them. You never know who will come through when you need assistance.[72]

The people who have the best relationships are the people who can adjust quickly to any career bumps in the road. For example, if your company goes out of business or merges with another entity, you may find yourself out of a job. If you have a strong professional network, you can access those relationships to learn about job openings and possibly even get a referral. In fact, I observed this many times during the recent economic downturn. Many talented people were laid off. The people who found new employment most quickly—and, in many instances, better positions—had great networks, which they accessed. People who took a long time to recover had no network to access.

Below are a couple of operational strategies for how to best leverage the connections in your network.

OPERATIONAL STRATEGIES: LEVERAGING YOUR NETWORK

- Build your network before you need to access it for a favor.
- Deepen relationships with people you know and meet people in their networks. Having a mutual point of contact makes it easier to form a new connection.

BENEFIT #2: REDUCED FEELINGS OF ISOLATION

Another benefit of having a strong network is that it can reduce feelings of isolation. As a diverse person in a White male–dominated space, you may not always feel comfortable and included. For this reason, it is essential that you develop a social support network both at and outside work. It's important to be open to forming social support relationships across lines of difference, but when you are in the minority, it's also very important to build supportive relationships with those with whom you share various identity characteristics (e.g., race, gender, ethnicity, LGBT status, etc.).

For an internal network, consider joining your organization's employee resource groups (ERGs, also called affinity groups). An ERG is a group of employees who share a common aspect of identity and want to associate with others similar to themselves. If your organization offers an affinity group or an employee resource group, you should actively participate. You never know who will participate in these employer-sponsored groups. By participating in these groups, you will certainly build and grow the relationships within your company or firm. The group could also be a great source of informal mentors and/or sponsors, depending on who participates in the group.

For an external network, consider joining professional organizations that share an aspect of your identity. In these networks, you can discuss issues relevant to thriving and not just surviving in your work environment. Regardless of whether your network operates inside or outside your company, it's important to be able to connect to those networks to realize you are not alone in your experience. Remember to invest time and effort in these relationships in the same way you put time and effort into your work projects. Both pieces are important for advancing your career.

Some of my best professional relationships were formed in the Black Women Lawyers Association of Chicago (BWLA). In BWLA, I learned to lead a varied group of people to accomplish common goals. Working as a volunteer in a leadership role with BWLA was the foundation for lasting friendships as well.

Below are a couple of operational strategies for how to use the social nature of networks to reduce feelings of loneliness.

OPERATIONAL STRATEGIES: REDUCING ISOLATION

- Stay connected to other diverse people through affinity groups, employee resource groups, or associations.
- Build professional relationships through a variety of different activities in which you may be engaged—for example, alumni groups or not-for-profit activities.

BENEFIT #3: INCREASED LONGEVITY

Research shows that burnout (i.e., physical or mental fatigue due to overworking and stress) is an issue that affects individuals in many sectors. Across professions, 50 percent of people report being burned out. The burnout problem seems to have gotten worse over time. Compared to 20 years ago, people today are twice as likely to report that they are always exhausted. Interestingly, higher levels of exhaustion are significantly correlated with greater feelings of loneliness. This research made me think of the many diverse professionals with whom I've spoken over the years who have struggled with feeling comfortable and included in their workplaces—on top of highly demanding jobs. The advice I always gave them was to seek out more people like them, even if they were in different departments. Maintaining strong social connections has even greater importance in light of the finding that loneliness reduces longevity by 70 percent, more than obesity (20 percent), drinking (30 percent), or smoking

(50 percent). So build social connections to stay in this game over the long term![73]

BENEFIT #4: HEALTH AND HAPPINESS

Studies have found that social connections are linked to stronger immune systems at a cellular level, lowered likelihood of catching a cold or experiencing acute stress, and reduced risk of mortality. Furthermore, social connections at work can translate to better performance and higher pay.[74] These findings may help explain why one of the most important factors in employee workplace happiness is positive social relationships with coworkers.[75]

GIVERS, TAKERS, AND MATCHERS (OH MY!)

As outlined above, there are many benefits associated with having a strong network that you feel comfortable tapping into. While you reap the rewards of your favors being fulfilled, make sure that you are consciously giving along the way. The rule of reciprocity is a foundational aspect of business and must be top of mind during favor exchanges in networking. If someone does you a favor, you must repay the favor at a later date. Professionals of color often fail to honor the rule of reciprocity. This probably stems from a lack of knowledge that this rule exists in business.

People strongly dislike people who take and don't give anything in return. Avoid falling into a victim mindset (always feeling like the one who needs help) so you are more attuned to the power you have to reciprocate. You don't want to be known as a person who is always taking and never giving. If you are viewed as that type of person, your network will shut down on you. Not only will existing connections fade away, but it will likely be more difficult to make future contacts because of your reputation as a taker. Nobody likes a taker.

Adam Grant, a business professor, buckets people into three groups: Givers, Takers, and Matchers. Givers are willing to use their time and resources to help others without expecting much in return. Takers look for ways to get more than they give in their relationships. They are never shy about asking for something they need and may not be there for you when you need something in return. Matchers strive for appropriately reciprocal relationships. They become Givers with Givers and Takers with Takers. In essence, Givers are generous, Takers are selfish, and Matchers prefer equal exchanges.

If you had to guess, which of the three groups do you think finishes on top? If you said Givers, you'd be right. Through their generosity, Givers are seen as more trustworthy than other groups and make their way to the top. Now, which group do you think finishes at the bottom of the pack? You may have guessed Takers. Although Takers fall behind as they lose the trust of those around them, there is another group that is worse off: Givers again! Givers, when surrounded by selfish people, overextend themselves by helping others and fall behind on their own projects. In an attempt to assist everyone around them, these Givers do their own jobs less effectively and put themselves at risk of burnout. Matchers fill out the middle of the pack. They follow the rule of reciprocity and keep their word. The only downside is that by keeping a strict score, Matchers may form transactional relationships that are not as strong as the deep relationships built by Givers.[76]

Develop a general sense of the types of people in your network. Be on the lookout for takers in your network and cut ties with them sooner rather than later. Also, make note of any Matchers in your network. These people may be offended if you are unable to repay favors that were granted to you. It would be great if the world were full of Givers, but unfortunately, I have not found that to be the case in the workplace. Therefore, it is important to be strategic about the people you keep in your network and to always keep your word.

I am a Giver. I believe in the laws of karma as well as "You reap what you sow." So I tend to be generous, but I do have a Matcher lens as well. When I help a person at the early stages of his or her career, I don't expect that person to help me. I do expect the person to help someone behind him or her. When I help a peer, I expect some type of reciprocity at an unknown date in the future. And I delete people I label as Takers from my network. Life is too short to waste time with Takers.

Below are some operational strategies for applying the concept of Givers, Takers, and Matchers to the people in your network.

OPERATIONAL STRATEGIES: GIVERS, TAKERS, AND MATCHERS

- Identify the people in your network as Givers, Takers, or Matchers.
- Align yourself with Givers and Matchers.
- Try to weed out the Takers who are self-interested and may try to take advantage of you in the future.

CONCLUSION

Whether or not you realize it, you are part of two networks already. Your family and friends make up your personal network, and the people you work with make up your professional network. However, if you have adopted a passive view of networking, your connections may be weak. To strengthen and maintain connections in your network, it is important to stay in touch and exchange favors. How frequently you do those two things will vary for each connection. By adopting an active view of networking, you can reap varied benefits from better health to more career success.

Rule 5

RECRUIT MENTORS AND SPONSORS

Mentors and sponsors are essential to your success. It is your responsibility to initiate and nurture these relationships.

It doesn't quite take a village, but breaking into the white-boys' club takes more than individual effort. No matter how fiercely you lean in, you still need someone with power to lean in with you.

—SYLVIA ANN HEWLETT

When I started out at a new corporate job in the Chicago area, I was excited and nervous. I was moving across the country and wanted the transition to go as smoothly as possible. I was confident in my ability to perform well at my given tasks, but I knew there would be a learning curve working with new colleagues and a new boss. Little did I know that there was so much I didn't know that I didn't even consider. To learn the ins and outs of the company culture, I relied on one of my peers. We were at the same level but in different departments. He was a seasoned veteran and had worked at the company for 20 years. He knew everybody. More importantly, he knew all the unwritten rules of the company culture. Since I was new to the company, this kind Italian American man took the time to give me advice on navigating the company culture as one of the few Black women at a senior level in the entire organization. He explained to me how my new company worked and what I needed to do to be successful there. I made sure to assist him in any way that I could to repay his generosity of time. In the end, he was a great mentor, and we became great work colleagues and friends. I will always be grateful that he chose to mentor me.

Another mentor I developed at the same company was a White male who was only one level above me. He, too, had been at the company for many years. He understood how to maximize the financial opportunities the company provided through exercising stock options. I had no clue how to evaluate and take advantage of this benefit, since no one in my family had worked in a company where they had access to stock options. He was kind enough to not only explain the process but to also reach out to me when the stock was at a price that made exercising the option a smart idea.

Both men were mentors across lines of difference who became very close friends as well. I got to know the people in their networks at the company. As you might imagine, both had extensive networks from working there all those years. You can definitely have mentors for different purposes, and you should seek them out intentionally with those different purposes in mind—you should not have a single mentor hoping that that he or she will be able to serve all purposes. Neither of my corporate mentors was a lawyer, and they did not serve as legal profession mentors—I had others for that role who weren't in the company.

BENEFITS OF MENTORS AND SPONSORS

You can be successful without a mentor or a sponsor, but it will be a much more difficult and painful and a slower process overall. Mentors have a wealth of knowledge that they have acquired through experience that, when shared, speeds up the learning curve for navigating your organization or industry culture successfully. They can also reduce mistakes made because of your lack of knowledge of the unwritten rules of your workplace culture. Mentors can vouch for you, which can facilitate your integration into the organization.

On the other hand, sponsors are in key positions of power and influence and are in a prime position to turbocharge your career. Both mentors and sponsors are beneficial to your career, but each serves a distinct role with some overlap in function. The key difference between the two types of relationships is what is expected of you and what is expected of your mentor or sponsor. In mentoring relationships, the energy flows toward you without an expectation of you giving much in return. On the other hand, in sponsoring relationships, in return for the energy invested, you are expected to deliver high-quality results. If you can deliver results, research from the Center for Talent Innovation shows that sponsors can help get you to positions of power and influence by increasing your likelihood of getting pay raises, high-profile assignments, and promotions. Sponsors take a more active role in your career than mentors do and want you to be successful because you become a part of their brand.[77] Later in this chapter, I lay out the roles of mentors and sponsors in even more detail.

Strive to develop several of each kind of relationship, not just one of each. Ideally, you should develop a diverse mix of mentors and sponsors, both at your organization and outside it. Think of this team as your personal board of advisers for your career. Each individual on your board of advisers plays a distinct role in helping you along your path. As you progress through your career, you will rely on your mentors for different kinds of advice. For example, junior executives tend to seek out practical rules and actionable recommendations to better themselves. More senior executives look for insights into their behavioral tendencies (why they do what they do) as opposed to rules.[78] Regardless of your position in the company, you need to seek out multiple mentors based on the goals you have identified and the type of coaching you need.

ORGANIC RELATIONSHIPS

You must be proactive in seeking out both mentors and sponsors. Often, informal relationships happen organically between people who share a commonality. In psychology, the tendency of people to favor members in their own group is known as in-group bias or affinity bias.[79] The most salient shared traits are related to outward appearance. Leaders will see less experienced versions of themselves in some employees, whom I call mini-mes. When a leader views someone as a mini-me, he or she is more likely to believe in that person's potential and is more likely to nurture it.[80] According to affinity bias, if you are a woman, you will likely have an easier time getting along with another woman than with a man. If you find out you went to the same university as another person, you will likely connect with him or her more easily. If you find out someone is from the same town as you or, better yet, same block, you are likely to consider him or her an insider. The more niche background details you share with another person, the greater the affinity. Affinity bias sometimes works to our advantage and other times hinders our ability to succeed.

From the start, those in the majority are viewed in a more positive light than members of the out-group, those who don't share the majority characteristic. That means that if you are in the minority at your organization, be prepared to put in additional effort to connect with your colleagues and leadership team. When looking for mentors and sponsors as a member of the out-group, you cannot rely on organically developing these relationships. You will have to intentionally seek them out and nurture them.

SECTION 1—MENTORS

MENTORS IN YOUR OFFICE

All companies have unwritten rules. Your ability to be successful depends on learning those unwritten rules. Research produced by the Center for Talent Innovation revealed that 85 percent of women and 81 percent of professionals of color need help effectively navigating their organizations' politics.[81] That finding highlights the importance of having mentoring relationships throughout your career. You should aim to identify an individual with immense knowledge of the inner workings of your company who is willing to share that information with you. Your mentor is a great person to inform you of those unwritten rules that aren't in the employee handbook. When you are starting a job in a new environment, mentors within your organization can teach you the unwritten rules of your office, help you understand the company culture, and translate the coded language used in your environment. They can also help you identify key players in your workplace.

That's exactly what my mentor did when I started my corporate job in the Chicago area. The right mentor also will be able to provide you feedback on how you are viewed within the organization. As you move up in seniority in the firm, you need mentors who will help you take your performance to the next level. The higher you rise, the subtler the cues that the culture provides. You still need help reading those signals. Individuals with a long tenure at your company or those who have previously held the positions of power you are seeking can be great choices for mentors. Through candid conversations with your mentor, you will have the opportunity to learn the best ways to navigate the organization's culture to achieve your goals.

There are many benefits to having a mentor; the trick is finding a good fit for you. You should look for an individual who has a longer tenure than you and is willing to take you under his or her wing. Having a good mentor should make you feel like you have someone else in the organization rooting for your success. These mentors also have informal networks, and they can give you access to those networks. Through your mentor's informal connections, you can pinpoint and meet the power players in your office. Your mentor in the organization can introduce you to the people of power and influence within your company. It is important for those people to know you and for you to know those people. You may not be able to identify the current power players without the help of your mentor. More importantly, you won't be able to identify the future power players without your mentor's assistance. You don't want to inadvertently cross a future power player without knowing his or her position of influence. Furthermore, your mentor may be able to help you get high-quality and high-visibility work. You need both to be successful. Finally, and probably most intuitively, mentors can serve as sounding boards and trusted advisers to you. When looking for sage wisdom in making career and life decisions, you do not need to limit yourself to the boundaries of your office.

MENTORS OUTSIDE YOUR OFFICE

You can and should seek out mentors outside your organization who will be useful in helping you chart your course and achieve your goals outside the organization. Mentors outside your organization can give you a more objective, third-party perspective on tricky office politics you may be trying to navigate. In addition, you can be more open talking to these mentors about your career aspirations. There are certain conversations that benefit from an insider perspective and others that require an outsider perspective. For example, if you are looking to rise through the ranks in your company, you should consult a trusted mentor in your office. If you are considering a change in jobs, you should consult a mentor outside your company—at least for the initial exploratory conversations.

MENTORS ACROSS LINES OF DIFFERENCE

There is another important criterion for selecting a good mix of mentors: diversity. You should choose mentors both within your own cultural background and across lines of difference. Diverse mentors can provide diverse perspectives on the same situation. Most people would agree that, when faced with a problem, it is more helpful to hear five different solutions than a single solution five times. The same reasoning applies when selecting mentors. It is important that you have mentors of different races, different genders, and other different aspects of identity. Each mentor will give you advice informed by his or her personal experience. Each mentor views the world through a different lens. The advice gathered from these varying perspectives may help you identify nuances in your problem that you had not previously considered. By getting a more complete picture of the situation through information gathering, you will be in a better position to make a sound decision.

Below are a few operational strategies to keep in mind as you recruit your team of mentors.

OPERATIONAL STRATEGIES: BUILDING YOUR MENTOR TEAM

- Identify at least two mentors within your organization. These mentors inside the workplace should teach you the unwritten rules of the company and provide insight into how you are viewed within your company.

- Identify at least two mentors outside your organization. Mentors outside your workplace can provide objective views from afar and are great sources of career information and opportunities as well as work-life integration.
- When evaluating the composition of your mentor team, make sure you have mentors across lines of difference.

SECTION 2—SPONSORS

SPONSOR VS. MENTOR

At the beginning of your career, having a variety of different mentors is very valuable. As you progress from mid- to high-level positions in your career, it is important to have sponsors. It can be difficult to tease apart the difference between mentors and sponsors because some of their functions overlap. Both mentors and sponsors give advice, provide feedback, and make introductions to people in their networks. The key difference is that sponsors are people who have power and influence and are in "the room where it happens," to reference the *Hamilton* song.[82] They are willing to use their power and influence to advocate on your behalf.

It is possible, if not likely, that your mentor will also play the role of your sponsor. It is important, however, not to confuse mentors and sponsors. If an individual either a) lacks the necessary power and influence to act as a sponsor or b) is not willing to advocate on your behalf, then he or she is not your sponsor. So if an individual is enthusiastically willing to advocate for your advancement within your organization but lacks the necessary power and influence to support your advancement, he or she cannot play the role of your sponsor. If an individual does have power and influence and perhaps even thinks about your work favorably but is not willing to stake his or her reputation on advocating for your advancement, he or she is not your sponsor. Finding the right combination of power, influence, and willingness to advocate is crucial for advancing to higher-level positions within an organization.

Sponsorship is not a new concept. It has long been used by White men to fast-track them to positions of power and influence. In the past, a critical factor for sponsorship was affinity, which was used as a proxy for trust and loyalty. That is a key reason why, in the United States and Europe, leaders remained predominantly White and male. It was incredibly difficult for diverse professionals to break into this old boys' club. Although access into the old boys' club is more open now than it has ever been in history, it is no stroll in the park for women or people of color. Men are 46 percent more likely than women to have a sponsor advocating for their success; additionally, White professionals are 63 percent more likely to have a sponsor than professionals of color.[83]

It is important to note that it is likely your sponsor will be very different from you if you are a diverse professional within a White male–dominated organization. You need both sponsors and mentors to develop your career. Many companies have formal mentoring programs in which you will be connected to a more senior member of the firm to help with your career growth and personal development. If you are lucky, your firm may be one of few that even has a formal sponsorship program to help you get into leadership positions. PwC, Deutsche Bank Global, and Deloitte are three top companies with such formal sponsorship programs in place. If your office does not have formal programs in place, it is imperative that you take the initiative to seek out mentors and sponsors yourself. The more mentors and sponsors you have, the more successful you will be. To get better, find a good mentor. To get ahead, find a good sponsor.

Using Sylvia Ann Hewlett's Book *Forget a Mentor, Find a Sponsor*, I put together a chart to give you a clearer sense of the difference between mentors and sponsors.[84] Remember that both are important for you to be successful but for different reasons.

Mentor	Sponsor
Who...	
• Experienced person who takes a passive role in your career, offering you guidance and knowledge.	• Senior leader who takes an active role in your career and is willing to bet on you and your potential.
Stakes...	
• Low-stakes commitment. Often mentors are happy just seeing you succeed.	• High-stakes commitment. Sponsors attach their reputation to yours and know that you can both succeed or both fail.
Reciprocity Expectation...	
• Expects very little in return. Possible expectation for you to pay it forward to the next generation.	• Expects a great deal in return. Primary expectation is stellar job performance.
Type of Feedback...	
• Serves as a sounding board and often provides encouraging feedback to build your confidence and self-esteem.	• Gives honest, critical feedback on areas for development and executive presence.
Other Actions...	
• Decodes unwritten rules of the organization or industry. • Provides tips on navigating the organization's culture. • Helps you figure out your life plans. • Offers empathetic support and a shoulder to cry on.	• Advocates for your next promotion. • Gives you stretch assignments. • Provides "air cover" so you can take risks (room to fail). • Promotes your visibility within the organization. • Connects you to senior leaders.

THE BENEFITS OF HAVING A SPONSOR

Mentors can have varying levels of engagement. Some mentors are passive and provide counsel only when approached. Other mentors are more active and check in on your progress periodically. Sponsors go even further and serve as active advocates for you. One of the main reasons sponsors advocate for their protégés (the analog to mentees in mentoring relationships) is because sponsors look good when their protégés are successful.

With sponsors taking on such active roles, there is a positive effect on the junior professionals they take on as protégés. Men, women, and professionals of color with sponsors are more likely to be satisfied with their rate of advancement than their peers without sponsors. In addition, full-time working mothers with sponsors are more likely to continue working than those without sponsors.[85] A sponsor's backing empowers professionals to stay in the game and play it more strategically. For example, both men and women are more likely to ask for pay raises and stretch assignments with a sponsor in their corner. Although sponsors provide many benefits, these relationships can be difficult to cultivate. Just 19 percent of male professionals and 13 percent of female professionals at large organizations reported having a sponsor.[86]

BUILDING YOUR SPONSOR TEAM

When looking for sponsors, the name of the game is clout. Look to identify the people who have power and influence in the circles you want to join. As a rule of thumb, sponsors are typically two or more levels above you. If you work in a large organization, follow the "2 + 1 rule" created by Sylvia Ann Hewlett, researcher in the field of sponsorship. Aim to attract two sponsors within your organization and one outside your organization.[87] If you work in a smaller organization, strive to have at least two sponsors, one inside and one outside your organization. The key piece of advice is not to put all your eggs into one basket. Having a sponsor who oversees your work area increases your chances of advancement in your current position while having a sponsor further removed allows you to keep your options open if you decide to make a change.

On their quest for sponsors, there are two common mistakes people make.

MISTAKE #1: CONFUSING SUPPORTERS AND SPONSORS

When the Center for Talent Innovation (CTI) asked professionals if they had a sponsor, more than 40 percent of respondents across the board said yes. The researchers decided to follow up by asking the same question but this time providing a list of the common actions of a sponsor. (See above.) When the role of sponsor was clearly defined, the percentages dropped for two groups. Only 13 percent of female professionals and just 8 percent of professionals of color reported having a true sponsor.[88] From these findings, it is clear that many working professionals may have the false sense of having a sponsor. To be clear, a sponsor is different from a supporter. Think of a supporter as someone who says nice things about you and your work. But remember, for a senior leader, giving you a compliment is low stakes. What really counts is when that senior leader puts his or her reputation on the line because he or she believes in you and the work you do. All talk and no action places an individual firmly in the supporter camp. Make an honest assessment of your situation and identify which leaders are supporters and which ones are sponsors. If you know that promotion discussions are coming up, ask your sponsor if he or she will advocate for you. If that person says no, at least you know that he or she is not your sponsor, and you can seek to develop that relationship with someone else.

MISTAKE #2: LOOKING FOR ROLE MODELS

When you start your search for sponsors, an intuitive place to start may be leaders in the organization whom you admire. The people you admire, however, may not be the ones in power. Professionals sometimes mistakenly equate the terms *role model* and *sponsor*. Research from CTI shows that 56 percent of women and 52 percent of multicultural professionals look for sponsors who have a leadership style they admire. This ultimately limits the pool of potential sponsors from which diverse professionals can choose.

In my experience, many diverse professionals want to be inclusive leaders who make everyone feel valued, but CTI research shows that only 28 percent of men and women in the U.S. workforce believe that their organization's leadership embodies a collaborative and inclusive management style. These professionals reported that the dominant style of leadership in close to two thirds of organizations is either a command-and-control, military style (45 percent) or a competitive, bottom-line-above-all-else style (20 percent). Since leadership styles can vary widely, when looking for sponsors, look for people at the top with power and influence regardless of their leadership style. Do not make the mistake of equating the terms *sponsor* and *role model*. After your sponsor helps you secure a top job, you do not need to emulate his or her style of management. You can exhibit your own leadership style once you make it to the top. It's just a matter of getting there.[89]

A WORD OF CAUTION AROUND SPONSORSHIP

Unfortunately, women face an additional challenge in finding sponsors. Often the individuals with power and influence tend to be older men. Sponsor relationships between older, married men and younger, single women can lead to speculation of an affair taking place. Even if both parties are married, the possibility of rumors does not go away. Because sponsors advocate for their protégés' advancement, people in the organization may entertain the notion that a romantic relationship or sexual favors are behind career-benefiting opportunities. With the knowledge that a rumor of an illicit relationship could be damaging to one's long-standing reputation, men in positions of power and women in need of

an advocate will sometimes intentionally avoid these mutually beneficial relationships. With the knowledge that people will likely judge the
nature of your interactions, it is important to have a transparent, professional relationship with your sponsor. Don't let the possibility of rumors
dissuade you from forming these beneficial professional relationships.

NO MIXING, NO MINGLING

Supporting the notion that men and women have not figured out how
to socialize in a professional setting, a new poll of nearly 5,300 individuals conducted by Morning Consult shows most people avoid one-on-one
interactions with members of the opposite sex. The poll asked whether
it was appropriate or inappropriate to engage in certain activities one
on one with a member of the opposite sex who isn't the respondent's
spouse: 60 percent of women and 48 percent of men responded that it
was inappropriate to have drinks one on one, and 53 percent of women
and 45 percent of men deemed a one-on-one dinner to be inappropriate.
Understandably, dinner and drinks may be viewed as taboo because they
are also popular date options. Since it is easy to conflate the two, individuals may avoid these situations altogether. The trend, however, continues
with lunch and work meetings; 44 percent of women and 36 percent of
men viewed a one-on-one lunch as inappropriate while nearly a quarter of
both men and women viewed a one-on-one work meeting as inappropriate. Simply put, many people are concerned with one-on-one time with
members of the opposite gender for fear of what others may say.[90]

I have often traveled with men for work throughout the United
States and on long trips to London, Tokyo, and Paris. I have never
thought of these business trips as anything but business trips, and none
of the men I traveled with ever acted inappropriately in any way. On
the other hand, we are currently experiencing a large number of sexual harassment allegations in a variety of workplaces, which have been
overwhelmingly instances of powerful males asserting their positions of
power and influence over younger, less powerful women. So it is clear

that these one-on-one business situations could have gone in another direction. What should women do?

With more men than women in leadership positions, avoidance of one-on-one situations with members of the opposite sex disproportionately affects women. Avoidance means women have fewer opportunities to build meaningful relationships with their male managers and to grow their networks with male colleagues through out-of-office activities like a catch-up meal. In the absence of formal mentorship and sponsorship programs, the careers of many talented women are doomed to stall. Whether or not it is happening, the perception of an illicit affair can be damaging for both the sponsor and the protégé. As a result, most senior men (64 percent) are hesitant to interact one on one with a younger woman.[91] When a junior woman is given plum assignments and opportunities for advancement by her senior male boss, her peers begin to question the nature of the relationship. If you are a woman in the fortunate position to have a sponsor who is advocating for you, you will be thrust into the spotlight with all its positive and negative consequences. If your peers question the attention shown to you by your boss, they are implying that you don't deserve it based on the merits of your work. Instead of shying away from the spotlight, own it. Be confident that you are not doing anything wrong. Be ready to articulate your value, but don't spend too much time defending yourself or justifying the increase in responsibility. Just continue to deliver high-quality work.

Below are some wise strategies for forming a professional relationship with your sponsor that I've compiled from the advice of others and my own experiences.

OPERATIONAL STRATEGIES: BUILDING YOUR SPONSOR TEAM

- Be mindful of how your words, wardrobe, and behavior will be perceived.

- Refrain from flirting, sending mixed signals, and wearing revealing cocktail attire for out-of-office events.
- Whenever grabbing coffee or a meal, meet in a public space in or around your office.
- Avoid settings that can be construed as romantic (e.g., dimly lit restaurants).
- Carefully consider the time when scheduling a catch-up session, especially minimizing late-night communications in person or over the phone.
- Schedule breakfast meetings at the office or at a nearby restaurant—less likely to be misunderstood.
- Schedule meetings in the office after the workday calls have ended around 5:30 or 6:00 p.m.—but not too late.
- Ask a sponsor out to drinks or a meal in a group setting. You could make a joint ask with one or two other colleagues in your office. A group outing is less likely to be perceived as romantic. The downside, of course, is that the sponsor's attention is divided among more people.
- Make it clear that you have fulfilling personal relationships and you are solely looking for professional guidance.
- Get to know your sponsor's family/significant other if possible.
- Talk about your family or significant other and, whenever appropriate, invite them to join your meetings or company-sponsored events.
- Avoid awkward situations—for example, attending a team-building event where you are the only woman at a six-person team event and the activity is renting a house and socializing and skiing—even if your sponsor is present.
- Participate in your company's formal mentoring or sponsorship program if you have the opportunity. Expectations are clear, and it is less likely that things will be misunderstood.

SECTION 3—MENTEE/PROTÉGÉ/YOU

At this point, after learning about all these benefits, you are probably ready go out and start forming relationships with potential mentors and sponsors. It is important to recognize that there are two phases in these relationships: initiation and nurturing.

RECRUITING MENTORS AND SPONSORS

Before you form the relationships that will be most beneficial to you and your career, you should have a clear idea of your goals and vision of your future. When you meet with potential mentors and sponsors, you should be able to articulate your abilities and aspirations. Prospective mentors may propose a few questions you should think about as you continue on your path and offer words of encouragement. With prospective sponsors, you need to be proactive in driving the conversation. Connect the dots for the would-be sponsor and spell out the mutual benefits of a relationship. Share your career doubts with your mentors. Don't share those doubts with your sponsor or he or she may choose someone else in whom to invest.

The following are operational strategies to keep in mind as you form professional relationships with potential mentors and sponsors.

OPERATIONAL STRATEGIES: RECRUITING MENTORS

- Identify your short-term (1-2 years) and long-term (5, 10, 15 years) goals.
- Share your goals with your mentors and gauge what kind of feedback you get. Great mentors will provide thoughtful questions and positive energy.

- Ask prospective mentors about their life stories. Everyone has a unique story. If they are willing to share it, it could be a valuable learning experience for you.

OPERATIONAL STRATEGIES: RECRUITING SPONSORS

- Do a diagnostic assessment of your skills. Get to know your strengths as well as identifying a few key areas for development.
- When identifying potential sponsors, make sure you can articulate your value add to their brand and reputation.
- Identify the people who have the power and influence to help you reach your goals and take action to get noticed by them. That could mean working on a project with them or talking to them when you see them at events.

NURTURING RELATIONSHIPS: HOW TO BE A GREAT MENTEE/PROTÉGÉ

Acknowledge that you need to be a great mentee or protégé for a mentoring or sponsoring relationship to be successful. No one wants to mentor a bad mentee or advocate for a bad protégé.

When it comes to mentoring relationships, make it clear what you are hoping to get out of each conversation. If there is specific information you need or a decision you are pondering, be very clear about that with your mentor. This eliminates the guesswork for both parties. Trust will form slowly over time. To maintain that trust, maintain confidentiality in the relationship. Mentors don't expect much from you, but trust and confidentiality are two core expectations in most relationships. Finally, give credit to your mentor where it is due. If the mentor gave you good advice and it worked out, go back and tell him or her. Even if the advice didn't work out, give your mentor a status update, so that he or she can better advise you moving forward. The more data points your mentor has to work with, the more he or she can tailor the advice to your specific situation.

If you want to get noticed by potential sponsors, then exceed expectations and be reliable. Research from the Center for Talent Innovation has shown that sponsors look for professionals who not only produce exceptional results but also have a "can-do" attitude.[92] The best way to nurture your bond with your sponsor is to step up when he or she makes a request. If you expect your sponsor to help you out, then be willing to put in the time and energy to help him or her. Don't be selfish and then expect your sponsor to be selfless. Strive to create a symbiotic (mutually beneficial) relationship as opposed to a parasitic one. If you can become a reliable "go-to" person, your relationship with your sponsor will strengthen. Realistically, you will not be able to complete every request exactly as it is outlined. Demonstrate your commitment to your sponsor first by saying yes, then bring up an alternative plan of execution based on your time and resource constraints.

The following is a set of operational strategies for developing and maintaining strong relationships with your mentors and sponsors. Remember that your sponsors generally expect more from you than your mentors because of their high level of investment. Thus, be sure to pay special attention to your sponsor relationships.

OPERATIONAL STRATEGIES: NURTURING RELATIONSHIPS

- Ask for help when you need it. Don't expect your mentors and sponsors to be mind readers.
- Don't spread yourself too thin. Be available to help your advisers (particularly your sponsors) on a moment's notice by selectively accepting requests from others.
- If you run into issues with a request from your sponsor or mentor, go back to him or her with alternative solutions instead of excuses.
- Be open to constructive criticism. Listen carefully to what your sponsor or mentor says. You may feel a little hurt by the feedback, but understand that ultimately if it is constructive, then you will benefit from changing some of your current practices.

RECIPROCITY IN MENTORING/SPONSORING RELATIONSHIPS

It is crucial to think of mentoring and sponsoring as relationships, not activities. Make sure that your relationships with your mentors and sponsors are two-way streets—ones in which you give as well as take. This is especially important in your relationships with sponsors.

For example, your mentor/sponsor may not be up to date on all the social media options but may be interested in learning. You can introduce him or her to that while you are also getting mentoring assistance. Your mentor/sponsor may be interested in a particular subject matter area, and you may find articles that you think your mentor/sponsor would like to know about and share them. The giving does not need to involve money. Your mentors/sponsors are not expecting you to take them out to lunch or dinner *per se*. You can offer to take your mentor/sponsor to lunch or dinner, if you have the means, but it is not required. You may not be able to pay your mentor/sponsor back for all the help that he or she gives you, but you can pay it forward. Make sure your mentor/sponsor knows that you are grateful for the time and energy that he or she has invested in you and that you intend to pay that generosity forward, acting as a mentor or sponsor for someone else: another person of color, woman, or other under-represented individual who may not understand all the rules of the game.

Below is a set of operational strategies for how to be a great mentee/protégé. These operational strategies provide a good foundation for effectively maintaining relationships with mentors and sponsors.

OPERATIONAL STRATEGIES: BEING A GOOD MENTEE/ PROTÉGÉ

- Develop relationships with key people before you need to ask for anything.
- You need to give as well as take. Look for opportunities to provide something.

- Be willing to mentor others to pay it forward.
- Maintain the confidentiality of things your mentor or sponsor tells you.

HOW TO END A MENTOR OR SPONSOR RELATIONSHIP

Mentor and sponsor relationships don't always work out. Sometimes from the start, they are a bad match. Other times, after a period of beneficial interactions, the relationship runs its course and is no longer useful. If you feel that you are not benefiting from the relationship, there are a few steps you should go through. First, think about your goals and needs. Then assess whether you have clearly communicated these to your mentor or sponsor. Mentors and sponsors are not mind readers. If, after an honest discussion with your mentor/sponsor, you feel that you would be better served by moving on, then that is OK. If it's not a good fit, it's best to walk away as soon as possible. Prolonging the relationship wastes your time and theirs.

Always try to end these relationships on good terms. There is no need to focus on how your mentor or sponsor is not satisfying your needs. Instead, express gratitude for the time he or she invested and recount some of the valuable lessons you have learned from the relationship. You never know when your paths will cross again, so it is best not to burn any bridges.[93]

CONCLUSION

As you work toward achieving your goals, it is important to recruit individuals who can help you along the way. Supportive individuals with knowledge and insight become mentors. Advocates with power and influence in your career field become sponsors. The best mentors and sponsors believe in your vision and want to help get you there. While these individuals are important for your career success, remember that these relationships do not just go one way—ensure you are an excellent mentee and protégé and give back to your mentors and sponsors when the opportunities arise. With a strong team behind you, you will increase your chances of attaining your goals.

Rule 6

INVEST IN YOUR PROFESSIONAL APPEARANCE

Your professional appearance matters much more—both negatively and positively—because you are more visible.

I don't mind making jokes, but I
don't want to look like one.

—MARILYN MONROE

Before we even open our mouths, we make an impression just by how we present ourselves. As a visibly diverse person, you stand out more, and your appearance is more obvious. When you stand out as different, your appearance is more closely analyzed for clues regarding whether you "fit" into the culture. People look at your appearance to gain information that may support or contradict the unconscious stereotypes they may carry in their heads regarding diverse professionals. Your colleagues may judge your level of professionalism and bucket you into a particular social class by the way you dress. Therefore, whatever you choose to wear, you must consider how it will be viewed by others as well as how you feel about your outfit.

In this rule, I don't tell you how to dress. How you dress will vary by work situation, your position, and many other factors. What I try to do is translate for you the different choices you may make and how they may be perceived. The end goal is for you to walk away recognizing the importance your professional appearance plays in your career and of acting intentionally in what you choose to wear. In short, your wardrobe and hair are no different than the other strategies discussed in this book. If you believe it is important to be your authentic self and choose not to follow the suggestions for professional appearance I propose below, that is your right. I encourage you to be very intentional about your choices and be aware of the consequences that may flow from those choices.

FASHIONABLE AND TRENDY EXCEPTIONS TO THE RULE

It is important to acknowledge that different industries have different standards of dress. If you work in the fashion industry, it is more important to be fashionably on trend. You will likely have knowledge of and try to implement the latest trends in your wardrobe, no matter how eccentric the style may appear to the masses. In the millennial start-up industry, the dress code is more casual than in corporate offices. So, if you wear a suit on a normal day in the office, people may view you as a stiff, uptight individual as opposed to a creative, disruptive innovator. Or they may think you have a job interview somewhere. Additionally, if you work in tech, it is important to be up to date with the latest technology. You may accessorize your jeans and a T-shirt with an Apple or Android watch or wireless headphones. In more traditional office settings, it is not as important to be fashionably trendy. The discussion in this chapter will focus on professional settings where business or business casual are the norm.

THINGS THAT ARE *NOT* APPROPRIATE

Fortune released an article in July 2017 on the 'no sleeveless' dress code being enforced by the U.S. House of Representatives under Speaker of the House Paul Ryan. Numerous reporters have been barred from the Speaker's Lobby for wearing sleeveless dresses. Gym shoes and open-toe shoes reportedly have also been banned, although no official dress code exists.[94] This latest news story adds to the mystique of what qualifies as appropriate business attire, especially in the summertime with increasingly hotter temperatures. Although Congress's dress code may be a little behind the times, there are rules—both written and unwritten—that need to be followed. Michelle Obama frequently wore sleeveless dresses as she redefined the look of a First Lady of the United States and became a national fashion icon. Although stylish and elegant, many of the former First Lady's outfits cannot be worn by women in Congress if they want to be taken seriously by their male colleagues. There is a misconception that if a woman is too fashionable, she must not be taking her job seriously. For millennials, the *Fortune* article demonstrates that the old Baby Boomer rules still govern a lot of workplaces—like it or not.

Most law, consulting, and other professional services firms have a business or a business-casual dress code. Although it can be difficult to decode the exact meaning of business casual in your office, there are some clear mistakes that you should avoid.

The following items are generally considered inappropriate for a professional setting:

- Flip-flops
- Visible body piercings and tattoos
- Long fingernails
- Clothes that are too tight or too loose

- Low-cut blouses and tops
- Halter tops
- Skirts and dresses that are too short
- Tops that expose the stomach
- Shorts

Some of these definitions are subjective in nature. Different people may have different interpretations of what constitutes *short, low cut,* or *too tight.* Although you may have a hard time defining these subjective terms, the concluding sentiment is that you know it looks off when you see it. As a clue, look to people who are in roles one or two levels above yours. That is a good indicator of what the culture expects or requires for you to get to that level. You can also ask someone you trust who is in a higher position, like a mentor. In this instance, you should ask someone of the same gender since he or she is more likely to be able to translate for you what is acceptable in the office culture. You may also ask the Human Resources Department, which can let you know both the official and the unofficial policies.

One of my friends at a large law firm has hired young women who just graduated from college or are in law school as summer interns. What some of these women in their 20s wore to work was clearly not appropriate in a law firm setting. To further exacerbate the problem, the women did not realize that there was a problem with their attire. One woman—let's call her Kate—was an intern between college and law school. Kate would come into the law firm wearing extremely tight clothes. She had a small build, but it doesn't matter what size you are; tight is tight. What the law firm hoped would be a passing phase persisted. Kate was not alone; in a survey conducted by the Center for Talent Innovation, 73 percent of leaders cited "provocative clothing" as the most common appearance mistake for a woman attempting to climb the career ladder.[95]

To resolve the situation, my friend pulled Kate aside and had a candid conversation with her. Kate explained that she became accustomed to wearing a certain fit of clothing in college. With such tight clothes, Kate's appearance was more appropriate for a night out with friends than for an aspiring lawyer. Her parents were low-income, first-generation immigrants. Neither Kate nor her parents knew what constituted a proper look for professional settings. She didn't realize that what was fine to wear in college could be problematic in a law office. My friend gave Kate a gift card and sent someone to accompany her when she went shopping for more professional clothes. Kate did the best she could and received guidance while she was interning in the law office. Kate learned the important lesson that people will judge you by the way you look. There is a socioeconomic lens that people use to try to bucket you. How you dress serves as a proxy for social class, which is often used to judge whether you fit into a certain (often White male–dominated) culture.

Kate's problem originated from a certain type of look that was common and acceptable on college campuses. However, it is not appropriate for people to take that look and bring it into the workplace. I remember when I went back to Harvard, my alma mater, for a Black alumni reunion. After the alumni dinner, there was a party, which current students were also invited to attend. I remember when the college students came in, I was stunned by what they were wearing, especially the young women. The dresses were *very* tight and *very* short. I understood that it was a college party on a Friday night, but I hadn't realized the current trend of dress that was popular among college women. There were very few outfits that I would deem appropriate, especially for a professional networking party.

There are instances, even in college, when socializing and professional networking overlap, like this party put on by our Black alumni organization. At this event, current and future employers were present. In these cases, it is important to remember that your appearance still matters. Social and professional circles often overlap. It is especially important for junior people entering the professional world to keep this in mind. Recent graduates need to learn the difference between work and school attire as they make the transition to the workforce.

You should always be mindful of your attire at company events, whether or not they take place in your office. As millennials take up an increasingly larger segment of the workforce, companies are beginning to host more social events catering to this generation, often outside the office. These events are great opportunities to spend time with coworkers in a casual setting, but it is important to remember that these are interactions that can and likely will influence people's understanding of you as you build your professional reputation. Be especially cautious about company pool parties. Shorts and a T-shirt are more appropriate than a bikini for women or a Speedo for men. When it comes to office costume parties, it is OK to participate in line with the theme of the event, but do so without being inappropriate or offensive. For a formal party that can feel like a night on the red carpet, it is permissible to be stylish and glamorous without being too edgy. For women, once again this means nothing too revealing or too tight. For men, it means no outrageous prints for suits.

If you are ever unsure about whether or not one of these items would be allowed at your organization, as a guide look to the people in leadership positions at your organization. For example, if you are contemplating getting a tattoo that cannot be completely covered up by your professional attire, look at people in mid- and senior-level positions. If you aspire to hold one of their positions in your organization one day and no one currently at that level has a visible tattoo or piercing, then neither should you. One day, one of my junior work colleagues came into my office to show me something. She lifted up her shirt to show me her belly ring. I told her to put her shirt down and not to show anyone else at work. I didn't care, but I knew our work colleagues who were very conservative would not approve—and it might negatively impact her career.

Below are a couple of operational strategies for making thoughtful decisions when it comes to your professional appearance.

OPERATIONAL STRATEGIES: WHEN IN DOUBT, HOLD THAT THOUGHT

- Think carefully before getting a piercing or a tattoo in a highly visible place. Even if your current organization will accept it, consider the potential costs if you change employers or industries.
- When in doubt, ask your mentors or colleagues who have been at the organization longer than you about what is appropriate attire for different company events (e.g., beach day or holiday party). It is better to err on the side of caution and choose something traditional/conservative rather than trendy.

DON'T DRESS DOWN

Many companies today forego explicitly detailing a dress code in favor of an implicit understanding of appropriate dress encompassed under the term *business* or *business casual*. One word of warning: on the spectrum of business to casual, you want to fall closer to the business side than the casual side. With this room for interpretation, it can be hard to identify what counts as business casual and what does not. Although the term itself allows much room for interpretation, you should not use the lowest common denominator as your guide for proper attire. That means do not start wearing blue jeans, leggings, or gym shoes just because someone else in your office is wearing them. Some people may show up with holes in their clothes or with a ton of wrinkles, but for diverse professionals especially, I don't recommend using that degree of casual dress as your guide. I believe if you dress the part, you will act better. When I took beginner tennis lessons, I bought cute tennis clothes. They made me feel like a tennis player, and I played better. The same principle works at work. It affects your subconscious to give you more confidence.

LOOK TO THE LEVEL ABOVE YOU FOR A GUIDE ON HOW TO DRESS

I prefer to use as my guide people who are in higher positions. There may be some quirky leaders at your office with a unique sense of style, but defer to the majority of your senior colleagues. For example, Mark Zuckerberg, CEO of Facebook, may wear jeans and a T-shirt to work, but you don't see Sheryl Sandberg, COO of Facebook, dressing that way. Look at how your superiors dress, and try to emulate that level of professional appearance to the extent that your budget will allow. This will allow you to hit the right chord when it comes to proper attire for your office. Remember that you are fighting against stereotypes (mostly negative) and negative presumptions, so anything that supports those stereotypes will not be helpful to achieving your goals. Dressing poorly will diminish your signal of competence.

Below are a couple of operational strategies for determining whether or not your work outfits are suitable for your office setting.

OPERATIONAL STRATEGIES: BE CLIENT READY

- After getting dressed, ask yourself if you would feel comfortable meeting an important client in this outfit.
- Look to the senior management for a guide on how you should dress. Notice the style and brands of clothes they wear. Don't worry if you can't afford a $5,000 designer suit. You can find comparable styles at a fraction of the cost. The real secret is finding a tailor who can make any item look great on you.

DEFINING BUSINESS CASUAL FOR YOURSELF

Professional appearance in our present-day business casual world is more difficult to navigate than in the old days when everybody had to wear a suit to work. Business casual is vague and ambiguous. Even the term *business casual* attempts to morph two elements that traditionally fall far away from each other on the spectrum of dress. You need to define a business casual wardrobe that is appropriate for your workplace and is also comfortable for you. I recommend adhering to your organization's dress code with a little tweak up. By being well dressed, you will begin to feel a boost in your self-confidence. But the benefits don't stop there. Power is relative by nature.[96] We continuously scan our environment for context clues on how to interact with those around us. In your office, by being dressed up a notch higher than those around you, you begin to signal higher status and more authority in your organization. You will likely experience a subtle yet tangible difference in the way people treat you.

One note of caution, as you begin to refine your wardrobe: remember to dress within the context of the situation. Err on the side of dressing a little more professionally, but don't go overboard. If everyone wears jeans, don't wear a suit and tie. That's too far. Khakis or black jeans are an appropriate step up from blue jeans. Some places allow jeans on Fridays, and you can feel free to wear blue jeans, but they should be nice jeans with a good fit and without holes.

IMAGE MANAGEMENT: BEYONCÉ

In my opinion, one of the best examples of image management is Beyoncé. You rarely find an ugly image of Beyoncé in social media or even in print. I read that Beyoncé spends $1 million per year on hair and makeup and other self-care. Now, we all don't need to spend $1 million on managing our image. But we could learn a thing or two from Beyoncé's attention to detail. When presenting yourself, you want to make sure others see you the way you want to be seen. To make this happen, you need to invest time and money into your professional appearance. The higher up you are in your organization, the more visible you become. Looking the part is an important component of rising through the ranks.

The following are operational strategies for taking your appearance to the next level.

OPERATIONAL STRATEGIES: INVEST IN YOUR APPEARANCE

- Adhere to the company dress code with a little tweak up.
- Invest in two to three new outfits each year that are professional and make you feel good.

EXPRESSING YOURSELF: COLORS

The way you dress may be one of the ways you feel you can express yourself and your personality at work. Without uttering a word, you can make a statement. The idea of dressing professionally does not mean blending into your surroundings and losing your expression of self. If everyone wears dress slacks and a button-down shirt, one way people differentiate themselves is with the use of colors. Colors are very important in the workplace. Many people may want to express themselves with the use of bold colors. Variation in color is not necessarily taboo in corporate culture, but wearing loud colors, especially a lot of them at once, can make you stand out for the wrong reasons.

EXPRESSING YOURSELF: HAIR COLOR

This not only applies to your clothes but also to your hair. In addition to making sure you have a professional hairstyle, you want to make sure that your hair color does not stand out for the wrong reasons. For your hair to come across as natural, choose a color that can be found in nature, not in a crayon box. Choose earthy shades of brown as opposed to bright pink or purple hair. Although some industries are more lax than others when it comes to hair and dress, as you take on an outward-facing role, you must adhere to a traditional business look. So while many of your coworkers with internal roles sport trendy looks accepted by your company's open culture, if you are the representative chosen to seek funding from a group of high-profile investors, your look should be more conservative than the typical look in your office.

People in professional services should look like they are ready to meet a client at any moment. When you go to meet a client, you should meet or exceed the level of professionalism set by the client's dress code. Clients often have business casual dress codes. If your attire is professional business casual, then you are fine. A senior partner would not feel comfortable with you meeting a client if you are dressed for a day at the beach or park. At the end of the day, you want your clients and professional contacts to remember you primarily for your outstanding work and abilities, not for what you wore.

Below are a couple of operational strategies to keep in mind regarding the use of color to express yourself and your personality.

OPERATIONAL STRATEGIES: COLORS MATTER

- Be mindful of the color(s) you choose for your hair, nails, and makeup.
- Do a quick inventory of the work clothes in your closet. Are the colors, fit, and style appropriate for your office? If the answer to any one of those questions isn't a resounding yes, then it is probably best to eliminate that outfit from your work attire rotation.
- Develop a relationship with a personal shopper who can help you choose clothing that makes you look and feel your best. Most stores offer personal shoppers at no cost because they want you to buy more items.

I once bought a beautiful pale gray dress that was loose and comfortable. I would wear it when I needed to feel comfortable. My brother said I looked like a prison warden in that dress. That forced me to look at myself again. He was right. I gave the dress away. (I knew if I kept it, I would wear it again). Prison warden wasn't the look I wanted—no matter how comfortable it made me feel.

DRESS THE PART AND REAP THE REWARDS

Individuals given a white lab coat made fewer mistakes on an attention-demanding task when they were told it was a doctor's coat than when they were told it was a painter's coat.[97] Participants performed better on the cognitive task simply by thinking they were wearing a doctor's coat. This research demonstrates that we associate a symbolic meaning with the clothes that we wear. For success in a professional environment, you should dress in the clothes associated with success and higher performance at that job, most likely business clothes. The age-old adage "Dress for success" may have some truth to it after all.

The general assumption made about diverse professionals in a work setting is that they are less skilled and less powerful than their White male counterparts. These assumptions feed into the stereotypes that women and people of color serve as assistants or play other supporting roles to White male leaders. Dressing professionally can be viewed as counter-stereotypical and disrupt the negative assumptions made about diverse professionals. Being dressed like a leader will help others see you as a leader. If you want to be taken seriously, take the way you dress seriously.

In order to support my personal appearance, I created a team of professionals I could rely on and often created standing appointments at my desired intervals so I could always get in when needed. My team included a hair stylist, a manicurist, a massage therapist (to relieve stress), an aesthetician (for facials), a personal trainer, and a Pilates instructor.

You may not need a team as extensive as mine, but I highly recommend you create a support team to help you look and feel your best.

ANOTHER PROXY FOR STATUS: ACCENTS

Apart from the way you dress, the other proxy for status in the United States is how well you speak English and what type of accent you have. Almost everyone has an accent when they speak English. If you learned English as a second language, then you may have an accent colored by your primary language. Even in the United States, where English is the native language for many people, accents differ among people from different regions. People from the South have a different accent than those from the Northeast. The U.S. workplace culture favors some accents over others. It is important to note that accents are dependent on a reference point. For this discussion, the reference point will be the standard Midwest American accent, which is considered to be fairly neutral.

U.S. ACCENTS

In the United States, different regions have different accents associated with them. Corporate cultures only view some accents favorably. People claim that the Midwest accent is a neutral one because you can't tell where it comes from. The Boston accent and the Southern accent in areas outside their respective regions can be viewed as problematic. The "valley girl" accent from the West Coast is also viewed as problematic. Note that in all instances involving accents, the strength of the accent really matters. George W. Bush was from Texas. He had a slight Texas accent, but not much. He wasn't a "y'all" kind of person. If he had had a stronger accent, I don't know if he would have been elected. When you think of people running for office, it is rare to hear someone who has a really thick, pronounced accent these days. Most candidates have a neutral or light accent.

BRITISH ENGLISH

There is an old joke that Americans secretly want to have British accents. When Americans say that, they are typically referring to the traditionally upper-class British accent. For example, in London, there are at least two types of accents. There is a lower-class accent and a higher-class accent. You can hear the difference between the way Prince William and Prince Harry speak and the cockney accent you find on the streets. Both accents show up in the same city, not too far apart. But in England people read into this and use accents as a way to judge education, intelligence, and social status. People in London who come from poor backgrounds may have cockney accents even if they were educated in one of the better schools. They often have a hard time getting jobs because of the way their accent is perceived by those doing the hiring. On the other hand, the upper-class version of the British accent is great and sought after. For example, Africans and Indians in the United Kingdom who have the upper-class British accent are viewed more favorably than Africans and Indians who do not have that accent.

THE CLASS DIVIDE

In Great Britain, there has been a recent focus on increasing socioeconomic diversity in the nation's white-collar jobs. For context, Britain's top professional services organizations tend to hire disproportionately from a small pool of private school graduates who make up just 7 percent of the nation's population.[98] Most students who attend private schools come from upper-class backgrounds. Therefore, the majority of the workforce in highly coveted, high-paying jobs tend to come from the higher socioeconomic classes.

An analysis of the 2014 Labour Force Survey conducted by the London School of Economics Department of Sociology revealed that on average people from working class backgrounds earn £6,200 (about $10,000) less a year than their colleagues from professional and managerial backgrounds. This difference holds true even when controlling for factors like education, training, gender, age, and hours worked.[99] This analysis starts to reveal the subtle favoritism for higher social class backgrounds when employers are looking to fill high-paying positions.

There has been a recent push to address the lack of socioeconomic diversity in the United Kingdom's top professional services firms. A new Social Mobility Employer Index was launched to rank Britain's top employers based on their efforts to tackle the issue of social mobility.[100] Organizations are taking the initiative to recruit applicants from less affluent backgrounds. These individuals from working-class backgrounds are high achievers but lack the connections or knowledge to navigate the professional networks system. These employers are trying to shift the focus away from who you know and where you come from to what you know.[101]

Ernst and Young UK, a professional services firm, removed academic entry criteria for applicants and scrubbed resumes of social-class identifiers to minimize unconscious bias.[102] Another professional services firm, KPMG, realizing its motto that if something is not measured, then it is not addressed, began collecting data on its staff's backgrounds. KPMG became the first UK employer to publish details on parental occupation and parental education level, two strong determinants of social class, for all staff.[103] Part of the challenge is that it is harder to categorize people's socioeconomic backgrounds than it is to identify their gender, ethnicity, sexual orientation, and disability status. When you don't know what to measure, then it is hard to track progress.

Recruiting people from diverse backgrounds is just part of the equation. Once those individuals from less privileged backgrounds get hired, then the firms need to take some steps to make sure they feel included and valued.

MOVING FORWARD: ADDRESSING ACCENTS

If you have an accent that people do not find desirable, that can be troublesome. Sometimes having a strong accent makes it more difficult for people to understand what you are saying. If your English is difficult to understand, then your accent may be looked on unfavorably. Americans may want a British accent, but there are other accents they don't want to hear at all.

This news doesn't really help someone when English isn't his or her first language. Many first-round interviews for job openings are conducted over the phone. These phone screens serve as a test to see if you can be understood. If the person on the other end of the line can't understand you because of your accent, then you will likely be eliminated from further interviews. I don't like it, but it is how it is. If you have a hard time getting past first-round phone interviews, think about not only what you are saying, but also whether or not you have an accent. If you have a strong accent, organizations will probably want to see a writing sample. The assumption is that if English is not your first language, you may not be able to write well, which is an extremely important skill to have in most professional jobs.

The higher you rise, the more important the ability to speak well in public becomes. A recent documentary I saw showed that Princess Diana enlisted the help of a voice coach to help her overcome shyness and sound more like a royal during speaking engagements. Below are a couple of strategies for individuals who feel their manner of speech is holding them back from the full range of opportunities they deserve.

OPERATIONAL STRATEGIES: ADDRESS ACCENTS

- If you feel your accent is holding you back from certain career opportunities, see a speech therapist and look into accent reduction training.
- If you struggle with communication, consider getting a voice coach who can help you work on pronunciation, projection, and intonation.

CONCLUSION

Professional appearance is all about looking and sounding the part. Having the right look won't automatically secure you the top spot, but dressing unprofessionally may prevent you from advancing even if you deserve it. If people can see you in a leadership position by the way you dress, talk, and carry yourself, you are more likely to make it to that level.

Rule 7

STRATEGICALLY SELF-PROMOTE

Self-promotion is expected and required to succeed. Be intentional about self-promotion.

It's not bragging if you can back it up.

—MUHAMMAD ALI

Self-promotion is an important aspect of the U.S. business culture and is an important skill to learn no matter the industry sector in which you work. It is important for you to be able to talk about your accomplishments without feeling like you are being cocky or narcissistic. White males often naturally promote themselves. (I think they have been taught to do so by their fathers). It is how they get recognized and promoted within organizations. If you fail to learn the appropriate way to self-promote, you are doomed to plateau in your organization.

In my view, it is better to self-promote badly than not to self-promote at all. Why is that? In many professional environments, perception influences reality. If you are perceived to be excellent and successful, people will treat you that way. It is a self-fulfilling prophecy. However, most of the time, this is not the default perception. The default perception is that a worker is average or below average, unless demonstrated otherwise. We have discussed briefly some of the negative stereotypes people hold about diverse professionals in the workplace. Do not assume that others will recognize your worth just because you work hard. Your managers are busy. They do not have the time to think about you and your worth. People do not actively seek out the accomplishments of others. They passively accept the information that comes to them. In U.S. business environments, it is expected that you will highlight your accomplishments. In this type of environment, your unspoken accomplishments will be overshadowed by the accomplishments of your officemates who promoted themselves and ensured their good news was circulated through the office chatter.

No one will know your full value if you don't tell them. However, openly talking about your achievements may be contrary to your upbringing if you are a woman or person of color. Many people of color are raised not to call attention to their own accomplishments or intelligence. Many women, especially women of color, are socialized to believe that taking center stage is unladylike and improper. However, women and people of color who want to advance in their workplaces must promote themselves. Failure to do so will cause people to doubt their ability.

If your peers promote themselves while you wait for your accomplishments to be recognized, the people in your office may mistakenly conclude that you are less accomplished than some of your counterparts. This perception can have a critical impact on work assignments and promotions. In the business world today, it is important for you to be able to articulate your value. Self-promotion is all about knowing your value and being able to articulate it. If you want to advance, self-promotion is not a matter of *if* but rather a matter of *how*. Therefore, it is important for you to identify the methods of self-promotion that are both comfortable for you and appropriate for your workplace.

BUILDING YOUR PERSONAL BRAND: CONTROLLING INFORMATION

If you are repulsed by the idea of self-promotion, you may have an easier time thinking of yourself as a celebrity who is building his or her personal brand. That is really what you are doing within your organization. You are creating the image of the person you want people to think you are.

One concrete first step is to conduct a S.W.O.T. analysis for your professional life.[104] S.W.O.T. stands for strengths, weaknesses, opportunities, and threats. After you create a list for each bucket, use the strengths list and the opportunities list to create your personal brand. How would you want people to describe you in a professional setting? Once you have a clear image in mind, your ongoing task is to only release information consistent with that image. For example, if you have an image of a successful litigator in mind, then only talk about your litigation wins with your work colleagues. Save the discussion of your litigation losses for your friends and family. We all have insecurities, but we need to be very careful with whom we share them.

It is important for you to know your weaknesses and threats, but you don't need to broadcast that information to the world. You can discreetly address problem areas with a core group of trusted supporters. As a diverse person, you already stand apart from the majority. You will be observed closely, so make sure you act consistently with the image you wish to maintain—both within the organization and outside it.

I learned about the importance of managing my image from a senior White male trial partner. He taught me how to take a "victory lap" after I won a case. You go door to door and tell every person in the office how you won your trial and how great you are. This way, you solidify your image as a winner. Similarly, when you know in advance that you will lose your trial, you "lay a mattress." You go door to door before your case concludes and explain how bad the evidence was and how the judge was against you. That way, when you lose the case, it wasn't your fault. It doesn't hurt your image.

The following are operational strategies for identifying the key components you want to be part of the brand you construct.

OPERATIONAL STRATEGIES: BUILDING YOUR BRAND

- Think of three characteristics, traits, or adjectives you would want others to use to describe you.
- Create a concrete vision for your personal brand. Think about what your current reputation is and what you ultimately want to be known for.

IMAGE MANAGEMENT: INFORMATION GATHERING

Image management is at its core information management. In order to control the information that feeds into your image, you need to actively disseminate information consistent with your goal image and gather feedback on what your current image is in the office. This cycle of self-promotion and feedback evaluation is a never-ending process. Don't assume you know what your reputation is in your organization based on what people have said to you directly. It is important to know what is being said about you when you are not in the room to know how you are truly perceived by people in your office.

An important rule of thumb here is not to worry about outlier opinions. You cannot please everyone. Focus instead on recurring patterns and themes when getting feedback. For example, if one person comments on your communication style, make note of it but don't obsess over it. If many people start to give you similar feedback, you should find a way to address it. There are many sources of information. Some examples are your workplace mentor or your peers. Be open to information from a variety of sources because you never know where valuable feedback will come from.

When I worked at a corporation, there was a coffee cart in the lunch-room. The woman who worked at the coffee cart, Sarah, was a friend of mine. I always talked to her as I waited for my coffee. Over the course of many short chats, we got to know each other quite well. One day, Sarah said, "You know, Sharon, the big boys are talking about you."

I was intrigued and slightly caught off guard by her statement. Curiously, I asked, "Oh really? Who?"

Sarah told me that certain C-suite executives were talking about me and my work while in line for their coffee. It was great for me to have this feedback from an unexpected source about how I and my work were viewed. You don't necessarily know where you will get feedback on your image, but be open to it from a variety of sources.

The following are operational strategies for gathering information about how your brand is perceived so you can tailor the information you disseminate.

OPERATIONAL STRATEGIES: INFORMATION GATHERING

- Ask reliable sources about how people perceive you in the office. Compare and contrast this perception to your ideal goal. Identify the gaps you need to fill or misconceptions you want to change.
- Identify the people in your office with the best reputations. What sets them apart from the rest of the group? In different offices, people value different traits. Find ways to incorporate highly valued traits into your brand.

IMAGE MANAGEMENT: DISSEMINATING INFORMATION

After gathering information, you should evaluate if people's perception of you matches your goal image. This is a simple yes or no question.

More often than not, the answer will be no. If this is the case, identify the misconceptions or gaps in information between people's perception and your envisioned reality. In some cases, people may have false information, which you must take active steps to correct. In other cases, people may think of you as a good worker but may not know the full extent of your strengths, accomplishments, or future aspirations. You must fill in these gaps in information to create a more complete picture of your image for your coworkers.

If people's perception accurately matches your ideal image, great job! You have successfully built the type of reputation you envisioned for yourself. Your work, however, is not over. You need to continue self-promoting and gathering information to maintain the image that you worked so hard to build.

Most people struggle more with disseminating positive information than gathering feedback. In the next section, I point out both large and small ways you can self-promote throughout the year.

DEFINING SELF-PROMOTION

Mastering the art of self-promotion is important no matter your field. Most people refrain from bragging because they were never taught how to do it properly in a non-offensive manner. In an attempt to avoid appearing arrogant, many people don't talk about their accomplishments and even go as far as downplaying compliments they receive. Bragging needn't be about obnoxiously establishing yourself as the center of attention. Instead, consider it a way for you to own and tell your stories in an authentic manner. Early in my career, I often downplayed my accomplishments because I didn't want to motivate or encourage my competitors. I wanted to surprise them. As I became more senior, I realized the value of building this armor of a great image around myself. This image protects you more than it harms you. Don't hide your light under a barrel.

In the following section, I have outlined eleven strategies for effective self-promotion. When incorporated in your daily routine, this set of strategies can have a significant positive impact on your career.

ELEVEN OPERATIONAL STRATEGIES FOR SELF-PROMOTION

1. Secure Your Insecurities.

2. Keep a Folder of Accomplishments.

3. Accept Compliments Graciously.

4. Receive Credit for Your Work.

5. Loop in Your Boss.

6. Participate in Company Events.

7. Form Self-Promotion Partnerships.

8. Elevate Your Small Talk.

9. Know Your Audience.

10. Say No... Because.

11. Create a Bio, Résumé, and Social Media Profile That Speak for You.

1. Secure Your Insecurities.

Identify one or two people in your life (outside of your organization) you feel comfortable talking to about weaknesses, insecurities, and problems you are experiencing. Reach out to them and let them know that they serve this important role in your life. If possible set up a recurring check-in to reflect on these topics. Many times, we are not looking for solutions to our problems. We really just want a space to vent. By simply talking about what's on our minds, we often feel better. Knowing that you have set aside a time and place for discussing these issues, you are less likely to blurt out this information while at work, even if it is on your mind. There are moments when sharing a personal story can deepen a connection with a colleague. However, these moments should result from an intentional choice to open up. Unloading everything on your mind when unsolicited can make those around you uncomfortable. These peers may form the impression that you are unstable. Family, friends, life partners, and therapists are better people with whom to talk.

2. Keep a Folder of Accomplishments.

A vital step in self-promotion is putting together an electronic file or physical folder that contains all your accomplishments and compliments received this year. The key to this process is that no positive item should fall through the cracks. Anytime you do something well, include it in the folder. For example, save all the e-mails you get from clients or colleagues complimenting your work. Do not rely solely on your memory when you have an opportunity to self-promote.

One of the most important self-promotion opportunities is during performance evaluations. Usually, workplaces give you a copy of the evaluation before you come into a performance review. Typically, a portion of the review is dedicated to self-evaluation. The self-evaluation is your opportunity to write down all your accomplishments so they go on record. It is your job to keep that folder of accomplishments and push it forward at the appropriate time so your boss can adequately review you.

No matter how frequently you get evaluated (e.g., quarterly, annually), for each evaluation period, whenever you do something great, store it in the file. This includes both quantifiable accomplishments like winning a case or closing a deal and qualitative feedback from clients or coworkers praising you and/or your work. When it comes time for your annual review, if you rely on your memory alone, you likely won't remember all the great things you have done. If you can't remember, then your boss may not remember either.

Sometimes your performance review is with your direct supervisor. Sometimes it's with a person on the review team who collected the feedback but didn't directly work with you. You definitely want to bring the file into your performance review to ensure your evaluation is as accurate as possible. If something is not reflected in your evaluation, this is your chance to include it.

When someone looks at your file, he or she should immediately know your true value. Over time your folder of accomplishments will grow. In addition to serving as a nostalgic reminder of all you have done during your career, the folder of accomplishments can also be a valuable tool when you are updating your resume.

3. Accept Compliments Graciously.

At times people value the virtue of humility to the point of self-deprecation. Nowhere is this more apparent than when someone downplays or rejects a compliment. People work so hard for recognition, but when they are finally recognized, they don't know how to react. The next time you receive a compliment, accept it graciously and don't diminish your hard work. When I receive a compliment, I always say, "Thank you. I appreciate the feedback." You can also say, "I appreciate the feedback" even to a criticism—such feedback can help you improve, so I think of constructive criticism as valuable feedback.

4. Receive Credit for Your Work.

Imagine you work hard to go the extra mile on a project only to have someone else receive the credit. Would you speak up? This is all too common in the workplace. On occasion, a malicious colleague intentionally deceives others to receive credit for work you did. Other times, it is a misunderstanding. Your boss makes the assumption that the person who delivers the news was the one primarily responsible for the result. That person, all too happy to be in the boss's favor, "forgets" to acknowledge the efforts of the other project contributors. To avoid this situation, make sure you call attention to your value-added contributions and receive credit for the work you do.

This can be challenging nowadays since many work environments place a high value on being a team player. It is important to recognize that self-promotion and being a team player are not conflicting ideas. With projects involving increasing levels of collaboration, it can be difficult to identify what each member contributed unless they speak up and take ownership of their contribution. Be sure to highlight how you contributed to the group's overall efforts. Also, remember to publicly acknowledge colleagues who helped you along the way by giving credit where credit is due.

5. Loop in Your Boss.

You should not wait for your performance review to let your boss know you are doing a good job. It is important to proactively keep your boss in the loop throughout the year. Work out an appropriate timeline with your supervisor for keeping him or her updated (daily, weekly, monthly). If your boss asks for frequent updates, he or she is not micromanaging you. Your boss just wants to know what you are working on to make sure what you are doing is aligned with the organization's goals. Plus, frequent check-ins give your boss a chance to make real-time course corrections before the end of the project. Any compliments you receive should be passed on to your boss or supervisor on a real-time basis. By providing frequent updates, especially of your accomplishments, you are more likely to ensure that your performance review is accurate.

6. Participate in Company Events.

Company events are another opportunity for you to build your personal brand. If you are a woman in a male-dominated space, the possibility of rumors of inappropriate relationships between the sexes can make it challenging to build relationships with your male colleagues. A company-sponsored event is a great place to interact with your coworkers. If you are a person of color, it is especially important for you to attend company events. Some White people need to socialize with people of color to feel comfortable with us. Just as this allows them to be comfortable with intellectual women or hard-working minorities, it allows us to show that we fit into the community structure and work culture of our professional sector.

Many White people don't know that many people of color. Noting that there may be exceptions to the rule, many White people don't have many people of color in their inner circle. Therefore, when White people interact with you, they may perceive you to be an outsider. Participating in company events will help you feel like an insider and will help others think of you that way.

Recognize that these social events may not be the type of events that you would choose on your own. Nevertheless, it is important to participate in company and firm events, even if you don't want to. For example, a lot of people don't drink, but a lot of work events involve alcohol. Many events are framed as cocktail parties or happy hours after work. If you don't want to drink, an open bar may not be very enticing to you. You don't have to stay long, but you should go and appear enthusiastic about it.

There are many ways to navigate company events so that you manage your image and time effectively. For example, if you don't drink or don't want to drink, you can go at the beginning of the event, order a non-alcoholic beverage, and leave early. As I said in "Rule 4: Actively Network," the important thing is that you show up for at least part of the event. Furthermore, being there at the beginning means more people are likely to see you and remember seeing you. At most company social events, few people are early or on time. Most people trickle in over the course of the first half of the event. In light of this fact, you are more visible in a small group at the beginning of the event than as part of a large crowd toward the middle or end of the event.

An additional benefit of going early and leaving early is that you avoid the people who are drunk at the end of the event. It should go without saying that if you do drink alcohol at a company event, you should not get drunk. My rule of thumb for work events is one or two drinks at most. Feel free to fill in with water to make sure you don't get drunk or hung over. Remember, as a woman or person of color, you are often particularly visible within your organization. Strive to be known for the high-quality work you do, not for bad behavior at the company party.

In large firms, you may have limited contact with those outside your immediate team, so when you are at these social events, make sure you talk to some people you don't know. Some people survive company events by hanging out with their friends the entire time. However, this wastes a prime opportunity for networking and self-promotion. Your friends are already likely to say positive things about you. And we both know that you are not going to introduce yourself randomly to a new face on the elevator or sit down to have lunch at a table full of people whose names you don't know. Company events attempt to create spaces that facilitate introductory interactions and strengthen bonds with your colleagues to foster a sense of camaraderie. At every company event, make a sincere attempt to talk to at least one person you have not formally met. In these short interactions with new people, you are in a prime position to promote yourself and to leave a good first impression.

There are some extenuating circumstances that should be taken into consideration when deciding not to attend an event. In the previous example of happy hours and cocktail parties, if you are an alcoholic, then the general rule of thumb is that you should stay out of environments that could serve as triggers for you. Recovering alcoholics shouldn't be in a setting with alcohol. In this case, you may want to disclose that information to a manager and find other ways to socialize at work.

7. Form Self-Promotion Partnerships.

Even when the opportunity presents itself, some people will still have a hard time promoting themselves. One strategy to implement in this situation is partnering with a friend who is willing to promote you. Identify a colleague or two in your organization and form a mutually beneficial promotion partnership. The way the partnership works is that you promote your friend while your friend promotes you. Using this strategy, you don't have to talk about your own accomplishments, but people will still learn about them. In return, all you have to do is promote your friend's accomplishments, which you may feel more comfortable doing than talking about yourself.

If you would like to opt for this strategy, you need to have an explicit conversation with your friend and not just assume that you have an agreement. Reciprocity is a foundational rule in business. White men know the rule of reciprocity well. Too many people of color, however, don't know this rule and may not reciprocate your efforts to promote them if not explicitly asked. Periodically, check in with your friend so you can update each other on your most recent accomplishments. You can also use those check-ins as opportunities to find out what is said about you when you are not in the room.

8. Elevate Your Small Talk.

Whether riding the elevator or waiting to grab a cup of coffee in the lunchroom, there are many moments throughout your day that are conducive to small talk with your colleagues. These small interactions matter a great deal over time. Take advantage of small talk moments by getting to know the people around you and leaving a good impression.

- *Conversation starters:* Prepare a thirty-second elevator pitch statement that describes what you do or what you are currently working on. You need to have a succinct and interesting description. Your response should serve as a springboard for further conversation. After being intrigued by the first two sentences, people will likely want to know more about you and your work.

- *Weekend updates:* On Friday afternoons, workplace conversations typically turn to plans for the upcoming weekend. Use these moments to self-promote and build your image. What you do outside work is a vital component of your overall brand. You'll know that you were successful if your coworkers follow up about your weekend on Monday morning.

- *Drop knowledge:* Stay current with global events and industry-relevant news. Sign up for digests of reputable information outlets like the *New York Times*, the *Wall Street Journal,* and the *New England Journal of Medicine.* Work tidbits that you learn into conversations when relevant. You will come off sounding well read and thoughtful instead of staying stuck in your bubble.

9. Know Your Audience.

A critical part of self-promotion involves being able to read your audience. This may sound counterintuitive. When talking about yourself and your accomplishments, why would you need to know the background of your audience? The answer is that the more you know about your audience, the better you can tailor your tidbits of information. Some accomplishments are impressive across the board. Telling someone you received the employee-of-the-year award conveys a clear meaning even if the listener works for a different employer or in a different industry. When it comes to your more specialized accomplishments, however, it is important to choose the ones that are relevant to your audience. For example, if you know your supervisor cares about the environment, you may want to mention the sustainability award you received for reducing the amount of waste your company produces.

10. Say No... Because.

As you get better at self-promotion and people hear about your skills and ability to deliver, many more work requests will come your way. It is important to strategically choose which requests to accept and which requests to turn down. If you take on too much work, the quality of your work may start to slip or items may fall through the cracks, and you can lose your reputation as a reliable, skilled worker. Sometimes when people ask you to take on a particular work assignment, you may be too busy. In these instances, it is important to say no, but don't just leave it at that one word. You may not realize it, but turning down a request is another opportunity to self-promote. When you say no, you can craftily weave in self-promotion by providing an explanation of the important matters on which you are currently working. When asked to take on additional work, you may respond, "I can't take that assignment because I am working on closing a multi-million-dollar deal." When you provide the reason you have to say no, people leave the interaction continuing to think highly of you and are more likely to return to you with work in the future.

11. Create a Bio, Résumé, and Social Media Profile That Speak for You.

Throughout this section we have been covering how you can promote yourself through what you say. Another extremely important self-promotion tool is written content. Your bio, résumé, and social media profile can all communicate your value without you having to say a single word. Have a mentor review all written content to make sure it fully demonstrates your value. You can also hire people to help you create bios, résumés, and social media profiles consistent with your brand/image. Make sure you also get a professional photo to go with your written content. You will be surprised how often you use it.

Speaking of photos, make sure all your social media profiles are professional and aligned with your brand/image. Nowadays, employers check not only LinkedIn, but also Facebook, Instagram, Twitter, and other social media accounts before making job offers.

CONCLUSION

In the absence of information, people make judgments based on assumptions and stereotypes. If you are a diverse professional, you will likely have to push back against the negative stereotypes associated with your identity. One of the best way to break down stereotypes is to present counter-stereotypical examples, and self-promotion does that.

If people start off with a neutral or negative perception of your ability, it is your responsibility to present them with positive facts about yourself so they can form a more accurate perception of you as a professional. When self-promoting, you are not stroking your own ego or trying to make others feel bad. Effective self-promotion is about being proud of what you worked hard to accomplish and willingly sharing those stories with others. Self-promotion is ultimately about owning your story and telling it the way you want it to be told.[105]

Rule 8

BE MINDFUL OF WORK-LIFE INTEGRATION

Balance is important for keeping you in the game.

Don't confuse having a career with having a life.

—Hillary Clinton

The road to the top is a long one. It is more like a marathon than a sprint. If you don't pace yourself and maintain a healthy approach to work-life integration, you may burn out. No matter how much you love your job, there is more to your life than the work you get paid to do. As you make your way down the long, winding road toward your goals, it is important to take precautions to ensure that you don't exhaust yourself mentally or physically. If you aspire to do well and be promoted at your organization, you will spend a significant amount of time working. While working, no matter how rigid the environment, find ways to make your job more enjoyable.

Ideally, you can do this by finding a way to make work feed your soul. If the work you are doing matters deeply to you and you feel that you are making a difference, then work will not seem draining. Your energy is a renewable resource. You can recharge by celebrating the little victories and the feeling that your efforts are making a positive impact on the world. Remember, you will never be paid enough to do a job you hate. You know that you truly love a job when you would be willing to do it for free. At times, work can be grueling, and progress will not always be tangible. However, you must be patient and engage in persistent action. A key component of achieving your long-term goals is resilience.

REDEFINING RESILIENCE

What do you envision when you think of resilience? There are a few examples that pop into my mind: a marathon runner mustering the energy to keep going at mile 21, a boxer receiving repeated punches and staying in the fight, and the employee who puts in 60-hour work weeks month after month with no complaints. If you are like me, the idea of resilience is centered around gritting your teeth, putting your head down, and powering through obstacle after obstacle. The values of discipline and hard work were drilled into me at an early age. It's not surprising to report that early on in my career, I thought that my self-discipline was the sole factor that determined my resilience. Over time, my conception of resilience has evolved. Now I recognize that the secret to resilience is the recovery time between periods of intense work.[106]

Most self-proclaimed hard workers skip the two essential steps of stopping and recovering when they have a lot on their plates. What's worse is that sometimes these workaholics boast about working nonstop in a self-promotional manner. Somehow over time, we have developed a culture in which a high value is placed on being busy. Research has shown that people believe in the twisted logic that the busier you are, the more important you must be.[107]

What most people don't talk about is that when they are overworked, their physical and mental health takes a hit. Research on occupational stress has found a direct correlation between lack of recovery and increased health problems.[108] In addition to deteriorating health, overworking can lead to a lower-quality work product. When you are tired or stressed, you are more prone to making errors and letting items fall through the cracks. As we discussed in "Rule 1: Success Is Intentional," our brains are hardwired to perform their best when we feel positive rather than negative or neutral. Actively prioritizing recovery periods allows us to remain positive, which in turn increases our quality of life and work productivity.

In the book *Why Zebra's Don't Get Ulcers*, the difference between short-term (acute) stress and long-term (chronic) stress is brought to life through a colorful example. Zebras spend most of their lives roaming calmly and occasionally experience acute stress when chased by a lion. The zebra's stress response focuses resources to core areas of the brain and body for better performance—in this case, allowing the zebra to run fast. While the zebra is running for its life, the stress response hits pause on "non-essential functions" such as digestion, tissue growth and repair, reproductive drive, and immune-system functioning. Although these are important aspects for overall health, they do not help the zebra run any faster. After a few minutes, the zebra either gets eaten or escapes and returns to roaming.

Humans typically don't have to worry about being chased by a lion. Instead, we have a host of other concerns like paying bills and meeting work deadlines that trigger a similar stress response. Unfortunately, these stressors don't go away after a few minutes. As a result, many "non-essential functions" like the ones mentioned above are not allocated the resources required to maintain overall long-term health. Over time, this chronic stress leads to a variety of health issues, like diabetes, heart disease, and ulcers.[109] To mitigate the effects of chronic stress, build in ample time for rest and recovery and avoid overworking as much as possible.

I should know about overworking. I have done it too many times in my life. In each case, the outcome is always the same. If I work too long without rest and recovery time or vacations, I end up sick. Sometimes it's just the flu, and sometimes it's something more serious. But in every case, it is my body's way of making me stay home and rest because it is too tired.

Recently, I learned that my cortisol levels were very low. Low cortisol levels lead to lots of bad things in your body, but one of them is very low energy. How did I get there? From working too hard for too long. What does that mean? Too many weekends straight without a break, not enough vacations, and a very stressful work life, including the stress of moving to a new city. So now I intentionally build recovery time and enjoyment into my life. You should, too!

INTERNAL AND EXTERNAL RECOVERY

It is important to acknowledge and implement two types of complementary recovery methods: internal and external.

- *Internal recovery* refers to the shorter breaks you take during the workday.
- *External recovery* refers to longer breaks you take outside work (e.g., after work, on the weekends, and during holidays and vacations).

Each type of recovery has a purpose. When you are at work, short internal recovery breaks can help stop or delay the onset of fatigue. These short breaks, however, are not adequate to allow for full recovery, especially not for mentally taxing work.[110] When you are away from work, proper external recovery allows you to fully recharge. By setting your work down and taking some time for yourself, you will return to the office with a fresh perspective and renewed energy.

VACATION? NOT RIGHT NOW

There are two common arguments I hear when I suggest that an ambitious professional take a break or a vacation.

- "It's not the right time; I have so much work I wouldn't be able to relax even if I took a break." Many of us have the impression that we need to complete most or all the items on our to-do lists before allowing ourselves to take a break that actually feels valuable. I know I believed the mere thought of pending work would detract from my ability to enjoy a break or vacation. Now I realize that life hands you an ever-growing to-do list. If there are activities that you enjoy, find time to go do them. Work will be waiting for you when you return.

- "Taking time off gives off the impression that I'm not committed to my work." This is a common misconception. Research has shown that people who use all their paid time off have a 6.5 percent higher chance of getting a pay raise or promotion than people who leave more than 10 vacations days unused.[111] It is important to recognize that the finding is a correlation, *not* causation. In other terms, taking a vacation does not cause a promotion. Instead, there may be a variety of other factors—increased happiness, better time-management skills, better judgment—common among vacation goers that affect promotion rates.

The best way to take a vacation is to schedule it far in advance and give early notice. That way, you can schedule work around your long-planned vacation, and people are generally very understanding. Additionally, schedule your next vacation the moment you return from the last one. It gives you something to look forward to when you are working hard.

THE RECOVERY MATRIX

Now that we have established the importance of recovery time, the next step is to identify concrete ways to integrate recovery activities into your day-to-day life to replenish both your physical and mental energy. The matrix below breaks down opportunities for recovery into four areas:

	At Work *(internal recovery)*	Away from Work *(external recovery)*
Physical	**1—Get Moving**	3—Athlete Mindset
Mental	2—Find Fun	4—Reflect and Connect

1. WORK YOUR BUTT OFF, BUT DON'T WORK ON YOUR BUTT.

We know that it is important to incorporate ways to stay active during your workday. Many jobs today require long stretches of time spent sitting and working at a computer. Sitting at a desk all day is not good for us. In *Eat, Move, Sleep*, Tom Rath presents research that shows sitting for long periods of time is bad for your health. More importantly, the research also shows that sitting for six or more hours per day considerably increases your risk of dying early.[112]

Below is a list of strategies for incorporating ways to stay physically active and healthy into your workday.

OPERATIONAL STRATEGIES: AT WORK—PHYSICAL WELL-BEING TIPS

- Take a lap around your office every hour to stretch your legs and rest your eyes. Use it as a time to say hello or connect with colleagues.
- Get a watch or smart phone app that reminds you to stand up and walk around when you have been sedentary for too long. My Apple watch gives me a little shock every 60 minutes that I haven't taken a step.

- Take a flight of stairs instead of the elevator or escalator. Make sure you leave enough time to get to your destination. When we are pressed for time, we often choose the automated option because it is faster.
- Keep healthy snacks in your bag or desk. Then if you get hungry, the closest option to you is a healthy one, so enjoy your guilt-free snacking.
- Drink water throughout the day to stay hydrated.

	At Work (internal recovery)	Away from Work (external recovery)
Physical	1—Get Moving	3—Athlete Mindset
Mental	2—Find Fun	4—Reflect and Connect

2. FIND WAYS TO MAKE WORK FUN.

There are some aspects of your job that can be frustrating and draining. Hoping for the project to end as quickly as possible is not a sustainable coping mechanism. Think carefully about ways to incorporate your interests into all aspects of your job.

It is especially important that you take fun breaks when your day is packed with work that you find unpleasant. For example, during the workday, you can spend as little as fifteen minutes brainstorming an outing for your employee resource group or ideas for an organization-wide community-service day. After work, you can set up social events with your colleagues or friends in the area. Finding time may be difficult because client and upper-management demands largely influence your schedule. Taking that into account, the more unpleasant your work assignment is, the more important it is to find activities that make you feel good and allow you to mentally recharge.

Another way to give yourself a mental break is to utilize opportunities to work remotely, if your workplace allows remote work. Working from home or in a coffee shop may be a nice change of pace from always dressing up and heading into the office. If you choose to work remotely, make sure that you balance "me time" and "face time." Me time is the time you work remotely. Face time is the time you spend in the office when your colleagues and bosses see you.

Not long ago, the primary way of demonstrating that you were working was to be in your office with a pen and paper or at your desktop computer. Although technology has made it possible to work remotely, it is important to make sure you are still connected to the office team. You don't want the phrase "out of sight, out of mind" to apply to you. Additionally, it is important to make sure the hours you work remotely overlap with those of the other members of your team so you can collaborate effectively. When done properly, working remotely allows you to take a break from your routine and still stay in the loop regarding work.

No matter how hard you try, there may still be some aspects of your job, like required travel, that can be unpredictable and grueling. You can only power through the unpleasant aspects of your job for so long. Taking a red-eye flight is a perfect example of grueling travel. They call it the red-eye because red eyes are a symptom of fatigue. You may think it is more efficient, but it really isn't. You will arrive extremely tired, and if you have a meeting or presentation on the same day, you won't be at your best. I used to take red-eye flights at the beginning of my career, but the more I traveled, the more I realized that an overnight flight is the worst way to travel unless you are going to go to bed and rest for a day when you arrive. Plus, you fail to make travel fun when you take a red-eye.

Below are a set of operational strategies for making the unpleasant aspects of your job more enjoyable to create a win-win proposition as we discussed earlier.

OPERATIONAL STRATEGIES: AT WORK—MENTAL WELL-BEING TIPS

- Find ways to blend work events with your interests by planning an event for your office or employee resource group.
- Utilize options to work remotely from time to time to shake up your routine and get a change of scenery.
- Be mindful about balancing "me time" and "face time."
- Go out for lunch with a friend or to network.
- Take a walk or two around the block to clear your head.
- Set up social hangouts after work so you have something to look forward to during the week and are not just waiting for the weekend.
- When traveling for business, try to reach out to friends at your destination in advance to schedule dinner or drinks.
- If you travel to the same city frequently, stay at the same hotel where the staff can get to know you and take better care of you.
- Consider staying over the weekend to have a longer catch-up with a friend or do some sightseeing. Spend some time in the new city exploring an art gallery, a sporting event, an intriguing restaurant, or a museum.
- When working on a tough project, explore a new restaurant or local attraction with colleagues as a team-bonding activity. You could be recognized for your morale-boosting efforts, and your organization may even pick up the tab for the outing.
- Avoid traveling with a work colleague who stresses you out. While team bonding is important, your mental health is more so.

I once had the good fortune to have a business meeting in Maui in the winter. Most people thought it was the dream assignment. Unfortunately, my boss decided to attend as well. Ten hours on a plane with him would have been too much for me, so I coordinated with his secretary and conveniently made sure we were on separate flights.

	At Work *(internal recovery)*	**Away from Work** *(external recovery)*
Physical	1—Get Moving	**3—Athlete Mindset**
Mental	2—Find Fun	4—Reflect and Connect

3. PRACTICE SELF-CARE LIKE AN ATHLETE.

You need to treat your body the way athletes treat theirs. That means eating a nutritious diet, getting adequate exercise, and sleeping 7-8 hours most nights. These three levers have a significant impact on your overall health and mood. If you neglect any of these areas, it will undoubtedly affect both your work performance and life satisfaction.

One of my favorite books is *Younger Next Year: A Guide to Living Like 50 Until You're 80 and Beyond.* In the book, the authors point out that evolutionarily, humans were not built for the comforts of twenty-first-century life. The technology and comforts we have today have led to a more sedentary lifestyle, which in turn leads to decay of the body and brain. The authors draw a clear distinction between aging and decay. While aging is inevitable, decay is not. Instead of trying to fix problems once they have occurred, you can implement a variety of interventions now to serve as preventative upkeep and slow down decay. The best intervention to combat decay is exercise, which serves as a growth signal for the body and brain. The authors recommend exercising six days a week—four days of serious aerobic exercise and two days of serious strength training with weights.[113]

Although many people say they would like to work out consistently, few actually follow through on this plan. According to the *Wall Street Journal*, only a fifth of U.S. adults get enough exercise. These active individuals have a few traits in common. First, they prime themselves to exercise with visual cues—for example, placing workout clothes on their dressers before going to bed. Second, they are flexible about the duration and intensity of their workouts. By not falling into the trap of an all-or-nothing approach, these regular exercisers can tailor their workouts to their energy level and the time available on any given day. Third, regular exercisers have a broad definition of exercise. Exercise can be any physical activity that gets your body moving. You do not need to get uncomfortable or sweaty in order to reap the benefits of exercise. Doing yoga, riding bikes with family, and dancing with friends are great ways to stay active.[114]

After working out at the gym and working at the office, your bed will be calling you. Ensure that you routinely get 6-8 hours of sleep each night. Sufficient sleep allows you to be at the top of your game. There exists a puzzling paradox between sleep and productivity. Many of us sacrifice sleep so we can keep working and maximize our productivity. The American Academy of Sleep Medicine, however, published research that shows insufficient sleep results in roughly 11 days of lost productivity for the average U.S. worker. The cost to the country as a whole is $63.2 billion in lost productivity.[115] That is indeed billion with a *B*. This research shows that you need sufficient sleep to get more high-quality work done. When we are tired, it can take more energy to focus and more time to complete a task than it would if we were well rested. By sleeping more tonight, you will set yourself up to get more and higher-quality work done tomorrow.

Exercise and sleep are important aspects of self-care. When prioritized, they will provide you more energy to be more productive. In the same way that you set aside time to plan your career goals, set aside the time to invest in your body. If you take care of your body, it will serve you well and for a very long time. Another key factor is diet. The food you put into your body is fuel for your body and your brain. Your diet is a fundamental aspect of life that has profound effects on exercise and sleep routines, all of which affect your work performance.

The following are operational strategies for how to better leverage exercise and sleep to increase your physical well-being.

OPERATIONAL STRATEGIES: AWAY FROM WORK— PHYSICAL WELL-BEING TIPS
EXERCISE TIPS[116]

- Invest in nice workout clothes and gym shoes that make you feel good. My motto: "If you look good, you will exercise good!"
- Work out in the morning for a mood and energy boost to start your day.

SLEEP TIPS

- Set a consistent sleep schedule. Identify your ideal time to start the day and work backward 7-8 hours to determine when you should be heading to bed each night.
- Allow your mind to slowly wind down at night by dimming the lights and putting away electronic screens an hour before heading to bed.
- Don't let your phone wake you up throughout the night with e-mail and news alerts.
- Try sleeping in cool temperatures. A cool environment can allow you to fall asleep faster and stay asleep longer.

	At Work (internal recovery)	Away from Work (external recovery)
Physical	1—Get Moving	3—Athlete Mindset
Mental	2—Find Fun	4—Reflect and Connect

4. USE DOWN TIME TO REFLECT AND CONNECT.

If you are an ambitious individual looking to make a difference in the world, your mind is likely racing with thoughts. When you live a fast-paced lifestyle, you have a tendency to lose touch with the ability to slow down and properly reflect. With the invention of the smartphone and apps, it is increasingly difficult to unplug. In the past, when you walked away from your computer, you were free of e-mails until you logged back on. Nowadays, e-mails are sent and received like text messages.

We have to make a conscious effort to manage the flow of information. Part of effective recovery is setting aside quiet time. Research has shown that silence restores the nervous system, helps stabilize cardiovascular and respiratory systems, and is connected to cell development in the brain region associated with learning and memory.[117] With all these benefits, it may be in your best interest to find ways to cultivate silence in your day. These moments may come in the form of short breaks in between errands, a stroll through nature, a silent meal away from your phone and TV, or meditation before bed or first thing in the morning.

A group of researchers recruited Division I college football players and provided them either mindfulness training or relaxation training throughout a physically and mentally grueling training camp. Mindfulness training (MT) included meditation focusing on the present moment and one's own breath. Relaxation training (RT) included progressive muscle relaxation exercises and listening to soothing music. The researchers found that all participants scored lower on cognitive and emotional well-being tests at the end of the intense four-week training camp. But there was some good news: the more an athlete engaged in RT, the less his emotional well-being score dropped. And the more an athlete engaged in MT, the less his scores dropped on both the cognitive and the emotional well-being test. So while both types of recovery were beneficial to participants' moods, consistent mindfulness meditation had an added benefit to the participants' cognitive functions.[118] My takeaway from this study is that periods of high-stress work will inevitably take a toll on our physical and mental health; however, we can reduce some of that toll and remain a little more resilient by engaging in mindfulness meditation. Although it may seem challenging to incorporate meditation into your daily life, it can start with a few focused deep breaths.

Choose the method of silence that makes you feel the most comfortable. After taking time to clear your mind, reflect on the events in your life. What has gone well, and what can be improved? What are you looking forward to in the near future? Have your short- and long-term goals changed?

After you have taken ample time for yourself, reach out and connect with others. This will keep you grounded and in touch with your authentic self. If you spend a lot of time in environments that lack diversity, you may feel pangs of isolation from time to time. To combat this feeling, spend time staying in touch with people like yourself. You may find that getting involved in a professional association is a good way to combine being in touch with people who share an aspect of your identity with furthering your career goals. As a woman of color, I have joined both minority-affiliation associations for lawyers and professional associations for women. These have been beneficial to my professional life and have also rewarded me with some lifelong friends and reduced feelings of isolation.

Of course, you may decide to connect with networks outside your current industry. Perhaps you find community through a religious or spiritual organization or a passionate interest outside work or in your neighborhood. The choice is yours. Just remember, no matter what industry you work in, you should cultivate quiet spaces and nurture your soul every week, if not every day.

Below are operational strategies for slowing down the pace of life to effectively recharge and become more resilient.

OPERATIONAL STRATEGIES: AWAY FROM WORK— MENTAL WELL-BEING STRATEGIES

- Block off time in your schedule for a walk through a park or other quiet space in nature.

- Stay in touch with people who share key attributes of your identity.
- Consider joining a professional association to connect to other people or a cause that is important to you.
- Connect with family or good friends.
- Have a weekly massage. It is both mentally and physically relaxing.
- Try acupuncture. It is important for keeping your chi flowing. (I love it!)
- Pamper yourself in other ways that fit your budget on a routine basis.

FREE TIME MAY COST YOU SOME MONEY

As part of maintaining work-life integration, it is important to focus on your home life. We all know that our work does not stop when we leave the office. Doing laundry, preparing meals, spending time with family and friends, and cleaning the house are all important things to do every week. If time away from work could be spent exclusively on recovery, life would be much simpler. However, even after we leave the office, we have other responsibilities. With a fixed number of hours in a day, our challenge is to figure out a way to stay on top of our work and home lives while leaving enough time for recovery.

Time is a finite resource. Although there is no way to slow time down or to extend the day, you can pay a price to free up some time. There are certain tasks, like cleaning the house, getting groceries, and filing papers, that you can pay others to do to get back a handful of hours each week while staying on top of your responsibilities.

Research has revealed that buying time promotes happiness. A wide-ranging survey of people in the United States, Canada, Denmark, and the Netherlands showed that money spent to free up time was connected to greater well-being. The same cannot be said for money spent on material goods.[119] Despite these latest findings, few people exercise the option of buying time. This does not surprise me. Like many others in my generation, I was raised to complete all my chores without complaint. Early in my career, however, I decided to hire people to help me to do the things I wasn't good at. Once I started, I couldn't stop. I hired someone to organize my files, clean my apartment, and decorate my apartment. Until I started buying time, I thought that only rich people could afford the luxury of paying someone else to do their chores. On the contrary, this research revealed that except for cases of extreme poverty, people benefited from spending money to free up time regardless of income.[120]

Be willing to pay people to do things that you don't want to do, like to do, or need to do. For example, you can hire people to clean your house. Having a clean and tidy space may be important to you, but it doesn't mean you have to be the one cleaning and tidying. By contracting out the work, your house gets cleaned while you can turn your attention to other things. With a clean home, your to-do list will be a little shorter, and your mind is more likely to be at ease in a clutter-free space.

If you dislike dealing with paperwork, join the club. The good news is that there are people who can organize your files and paperwork for you. I have paid someone to organize my files at home and in my office as well as my storage place. It gives me a sense of control to have everything in its right place. But I know myself well enough to know not to try to do it myself since I hate this chore too much! Feel free to delegate this tedious task and spend your time catching up with a friend or working out instead.

Another common household chore that can be delegated is shopping for groceries. There are many services that allow you to select your groceries online and have them delivered when it is most convenient for you. Furthermore, if you buy some items regularly, you can set up a recurring purchase and skip the hassle of logging in to order those items each week.

If you want to free up even more time by not cooking but aren't a fan of eating out every night, one great alternative is a meal delivery service. It's like having a personal chef but cheaper. Instead of shipping you groceries, these companies send you prepackaged meals of your choice from a set menu. These companies cater to a variety of dietary restrictions and feature health-conscious options. Grocery delivery services save you the time and the trouble of going to the store. Meal delivery services save you additional time by bypassing cooking and providing you with healthy food directly. If you have kids, be sure to put a baby sitter on retainer on the weekends so that you and your spouse or partner can go out without the kids.

All these services are offered at a variety of price points. The more you want off your plate, the more you have to pay. We must find the most efficient way to spend our time taking care of our responsibilities while also enjoying our lives. Time is valuable, and you should know that with some careful planning and consideration of your finances, buying time by delegating tasks is an option that is available to you. I strongly suggest buying time when you can.

Below are operational strategies for using your time more effectively by recruiting the help of others who are willing and able.

OPERATIONAL STRATEGIES: BUY TIME

- Be willing to pay people to do things you don't want to do, like to do, or need to do.
- Hire a cleaning service to clean your living space once a week or twice a month.
- Hire individuals who can organize your files and paperwork for you.
- Try a grocery delivery or meal delivery service for a week or two. If you find it useful, continue the service. If not, feel free to cancel.
- If you have kids, be sure to put a baby sitter on retainer on the weekends, so that you and your spouse or partner can go out without the kids.
- Make the most of your exercise time—get a personal trainer.

DISTRIBUTING HOME RESPONSIBILITIES EQUITABLY

If you live with a partner or roommate(s), make sure that cleaning, grocery shopping, and other chores are equitably balanced. This is especially important for women, who do more housework and child care than men, according to a survey of 34,000 employees conducted by LeanIn.Org and McKinsey & Company. The survey also found that people who do more work at home express less interest in becoming top executives. Only 34 percent of women who do a majority of housework and child care express interest in becoming top executives at their organizations. Among women who share household and child-care duties evenly with their partners, 43 percent aspire to be top executives.

It is important to note that the same holds true for men. The more work men do at home, the less interest they express in landing a position as a top executive. The number one reason cited by both men and women for not wanting to be a top executive was, "I wouldn't be able to balance family and work commitments." This sentiment resonates with many professionals regardless of industry.[121]

Imagine if work was split more equitably between partners. The important household responsibilities would be taken care of while preserving a few hours of free time each week for both partners. An individual could use that free time to recharge and gear up for the week ahead. It would also allow an individual to take on a stretch assignment or stay late at the office to go the extra mile on a project, which could help get him or her a coveted promotion. A more equitable distribution of housework allows both partners the opportunity to recharge and advance their careers while investing in a comfortable home environment.

As we reviewed in the "Playing Field" section of the book, fewer than 7 percent of Fortune 500 CEOs are women. When brainstorming ways for women to break the glass ceiling and acquire more positions as top executives, some of the initiatives need to take place outside the office. According to a report by LeanIn.Org and McKinsey & Company, women in senior management are seven times more likely than men at the same level to report doing a majority of household work.[122] By implementing a more equitable distribution of the housework and child care that has historically and disproportionately fallen on women, we may begin to see more women move from middle management positions to top executive positions in the organizations.

Balancing work commitments with family responsibilities takes conscious and consistent effort. After determining which household tasks can be delegated and/or shared with others, there will undoubtedly still be household tasks on your plate. Since these responsibilities are important, it is critical for you not to neglect them. Family responsibilities are no less important just because we do not get compensation or formal performance evaluations for completing them. Therefore, it is important to seek a solution in which household responsibilities are fulfilled while avoiding burnout.

RELATIONSHIPS AT WORK

Another area in which some people try to integrate their work and personal lives is romantic relationships at work. It may seem efficient because both of you are working long hours. It may make sense since you have work in common. But it is an extremely bad idea and a great way to damage your career and reputation. If it constitutes sexual harassment, it is unlawful.

My advice is to avoid romantic relationships (including sexual relationships) with work colleagues, bosses, clients, and vendors/suppliers. Too many of these relationships end badly for one or both people involved. In a few rare instances, it leads to "happily ever after," but the odds are not in your favor.

If you want to pursue such a relationship, then one of you should leave the company and go to work somewhere unrelated. If it's meant to be, it will flourish away from work. If you feel that a supervisor is pressuring you to be in a relationship, then you should report him or her to the Human Resources (HR) Department. You should not submit to an unwanted relationship. Gather any evidence you can, including text, notes, and e-mails, and provide it to the HR Department or upper management.

CONCLUSION

How you spend your time outside the office sets you up to play the long game. Stay in touch with your friends and family. Keep your body healthy and take time to exercise. Be careful about the use (and abuse) of alcohol, cigarettes, and controlled substances. Give your brain an opportunity to relax from the stress of your everyday job. Find ways to get in touch with your creative side. Visit art galleries, see movies, write, and read books just for fun. Finally, don't forget about time off from work. Vacations are essential—the longer the better. Try not to be an all-work-and-no-play-person. Spend time doing things other than work: exercise, charitable activities, time with your friends and family, art, dance, plays, concerts, religious activities—whatever you enjoy. Invest in season tickets for plays, concerts, or sporting events that you enjoy. These event subscriptions generally save you money and are spaced out throughout the year to give you break when you might not otherwise take one. Develop hobbies and other interests outside the office. It will make you an interesting person and keep you from suffering from burnout.

Rule 9

BECOME A POWER PLAYER AND PAY IT FORWARD

Use your power and position for good.

*Our lives begin to end the day we are
silent about the things that matter.*

—*Martin Luther King Jr.*

What is a "Power Player" in a professional context? A "Power Player" is someone who is held in high regard because he or she reliably gets things done. Power Players personify a winning attitude. Power Players are the "go-to" people and star performers in the organization who get tapped for promotions and leadership positions when they become available. When managers are putting together a team, Power Players are often considered first because of their esteemed reputations. The rules we have addressed thus far will help you increase your standing as a Power Player at your organization and within your community. Producing excellent work, always hitting your numbers, networking, finding mentors and sponsors, keeping your professional appearance sharp, and promoting yourself when done properly will help establish you as a Power Player within your organization.

BECOME AN EXTERNAL POWER PLAYER

One way to increase your standing within the organization is to be known as a Power Player outside the organization. If people recognize you as an important Power Player in the industry, it will not take long for your organization to notice as well. Traditionally, individuals rise through the ranks at their organizations and then take on highly visibly positions outside them. A Power Player generally brings good publicity or useful connections to his or her organization. There is no rule against flipping the script and using your external Power Player status to negotiate your way to greater responsibilities within your organization. Besides, sometimes it is easier to establish yourself as an external Power Player than an internal one. At the office, you are limited by the work assignments that come your way, but in the outside world, the possibilities are endless. You have more control over your outside-work activities than your internal work assignments. Therefore, to develop and display certain abilities that feed into your envisioned personal brand, look for opportunities outside the office.

At one point, I was in a role that didn't require leadership ability and didn't let me develop leadership skills. So I looked outside my organization for leadership roles as a volunteer in not-for-profits or professional organizations. I did this to meet my personal needs and develop my leadership skills.

One of the most important keys to acquiring status as an external Power Player is to be publicly visible. There are a variety of activities that you can pursue. The key is that the activity should increase your visibility within your industry. For example, you can participate in bar association activities, not-for-profit activities, civic boards and commissions, or trade associations. Do not think your work is done after joining a mailing list. To position yourself as a Power Player, you need to participate in events with the organization and volunteer for opportunities that give you responsibility and position you as a public face of the organization. Get involved by speaking on panels at different events, joining various leadership committees, sitting on advisory boards, and anything else that will make you more visible to the members of the organization. When engaged in external activities, you are building a public image through which people ideally view you as a "go-to" person. Aim to build a credible reputation, and people will solicit your views frequently. This means you must keep your reputation squeaky clean. (Your reputation is what people say about you when you are not in the room.)

BALANCING WORK AND OUTSIDE ACTIVITIES

Earlier in this book, we discussed how we sometimes find ourselves in jobs that are not completely satisfying. Even when a job offers generous pay, robust benefits, and job security, we may still be left with a feeling of longing for something more. In those instances, it is important to take up an external activity that gives you a sense of fulfillment that your job is not providing you. Your work must come first, but it does not have to be the only outlet for you to utilize your talents and abilities. For example, if you are interested in the arts but your job does not provide a sufficient creative outlet, you could volunteer at a local arts center, at an after-school arts program, or for the local art museum's junior board. While you pursue your interests and give back to your community, you will be interacting with and working alongside others who are also drawn to the arts. Whether it was your intention or not, you will end up with a network of people in the arts just by showing up and doing what you love.

The best external activities to take on not only provide a sense of fulfillment, but also align with your goals and your work. For example, I am passionate about the diversity and inclusion space. To view my work through a new lens and grow my network, I have taken on external activities in which I help advance women of color in the legal profession, advocate for diverse student bodies at top-tier educational institutions, and moderate panels on how companies are adapting to changing workforce and client demands. These volunteer external commitments feed my soul and inform my work.

As you search for external activities in which to get involved, try to find activities that align with your goals and your work, if possible. For instance, external activities can be especially useful if you feel you are not developing as fast as you would like at your organization because of a dearth of leadership opportunities. Often, bar associations and not-for-profit boards will give you an opportunity to shine and improve your skill set in a leadership position—long before your employer provides you with that opportunity. This happens because an organization with limited resources will ask people at all levels to take on more responsibility and give them more independence. Taking on leadership roles in external organizations gives you the ability to build leadership skills that you may not have had a chance yet to build at work. By the time you get a leadership position at work, you won't be starting from scratch because you will be able to draw from your leadership experience in your external activities.

HONOR YOUR COMMITMENTS

It is extremely important that you honor your commitments externally. With the notion that work comes first, some people only allocate time to their external commitments when their work is slow. Because of unpredictable spikes in work flow, it can be easy to neglect or drop the ball on your external commitments and then resort to damage control when work calms down. Although your responsibilities for an outside activity may appear to be lower stakes than your job responsibilities, you should treat those external commitments the same way you would treat your work. Your reputation follows you wherever you go. You don't want to develop a reputation that has people saying, "He/she never does what he/she says; he/she is unreliable." Although you do not receive formal performance evaluations on external commitments, people will form judgments about you and those judgments can spread. If you can't follow through on small projects after making a verbal commitment, why would anyone trust you with a high-profile project? It's a small world, and information spreads like wildfire. Your reputation is a vital key to your success, so try to be diligent when choosing your commitments.

GAUGE MANAGEMENT SUPPORT

How you balance work and external activities really depends on the nature of the external activities and whether you have management's or your boss's support for participation in those activities. Some companies and organizations may support the activities you do outside work and will allow and encourage you take time away from work for those activities. Some companies provide financial support for not-for-profit activities in which employees are engaged. You are always expected to get your work done, but as long as you are on top of your work, your employer may be willing to be flexible on hours. Some employers value community service and community engagement. Some employers do not value such service. Make sure you know where your employer stands as you take on external commitments.

GETTING OUT AND TIMING THE EXIT

After joining an external activity, you may find out that your goals and interests do not align with the organization's day-to-day operations. Because time is a scarce resource, there is no question that you should stop the external activity and find another one that is a better fit for you. It is important to thoughtfully weigh the pros and cons of honoring your commitment and your reasons for leaving. Most boards have two-to three-year term limits. If the activity is not an ideal fit but is tolerable, you should complete your term. When the opportunity to serve another term comes up, you can make it clear that you are not interested. You can use this opportunity to self-promote by saying no with the explanation that you have increased responsibility in another area of your life.

Most organizations also have natural reset points based on the end of the calendar year or the end of the fiscal year. These moments are also natural points when you can exit smoothly. It is important to preserve your reputation and not burn any bridges as you leave the organization. When I have decided not to pursue a second term on a board, I always work hard to make sure that the group will say positive things about me, rather than "We are glad she is gone." Remember, it is a very small professional world.

In some rare instances, you should exit immediately. If something illegal or immoral is happening at your organization, you need to get out as soon as possible because you don't want your brand associated with the offense. All the activities you are involved in, internally and externally, feed into your brand. You need to be diligent about maintaining and protecting your brand and, by extension, your reputation. If the leadership in one of your external activities is going to take a path that you don't feel comfortable with, you need to be ready to voice your concerns and, if the need arises, walk away from the activity.

I was on a board that gave out an annual award recognizing achievement in an individual's career. One year, the board selected a recipient who publicly made a lot of statements that I considered racist. I knew I couldn't have my brand as a diversity and inclusion advocate associated with a racist person. People would question my judgment if I approved an award for someone who openly exhibited racist behavior. My answer couldn't be, "Well, the board decided." That might have been true, but I still decide for myself what I put my name on. If you don't want your name and reputation attached to an event or decision, you need to get out. If it happens on your watch, it will be associated with your brand.

At the board meeting, I adamantly and unequivocally stated my view that the award should be given to someone else. Thankfully, I was able to convince the board to find a more suitable candidate. If they had insisted on giving the award to the individual I viewed as racist, I was ready to walk away. The sooner you get out of something that you know doesn't align with your goals the better. Thoughtful consideration of timing your exit should help maintain your reputation as you pursue other ventures.

CONNECT THE TWO WORLDS

Once you establish yourself as a Power Player in external activities, you need to find ways to bring that status to your organization to increase your standing internally. It is up to you to build a bridge between your external activities and your organization to reap the rewards of your effort. There are a lot of benefits to being viewed as an external Power Player by your organization. You can bring good publicity to yourself and your company. Your reputation can help you attract new clients and increase your value-add to the organization. As people recognize your ability and status, they will start to see you as a Power Player internally. This not only positions you well for promotions but also can provide protection against downsizing and office politics. Your increased visibility internally can be used, in turn, to benefit your external activities. This becomes a positive feedback loop.

Organizations regularly look for pro bono or social impact projects. As an internal Power Player, you may be able to direct your company's resources, financial and other, to support your external activities. It is not unheard of for companies to invest in causes that are important to their employees as part of their organization's charitable contributions strategy. By showing your commitment to and passion for a not-for-profit or civic activity, you might be able to bring the resources of your company to that cause. Your status in your external activities will no doubt increase if you are able to direct your company's resources to them. You can strategically capitalize on this cycle of leveraging your position as an external Power Player to increase your standing internally and vice versa.

Apart from building your credibility internally as a "go-to" person, being a Power Player externally can be useful when you decide it's time to leave your firm. Imagine entering a job market in which people outside your office already think of you as a star performer. If you properly position yourself as an external Power Player, employers will be waiting to snatch you up because of your stellar reputation.

Below are operational strategies you can use to increase your standing as a Power Player by taking on more responsibility both within and outside your organization.

OPERATIONAL STRATEGIES: BEING A POWER PLAYER

- Look to find whatever your job lacks through activities outside of work (e.g., not-for-profit boards, bar associations, civic activities, etc.).
- Treat external commitments with the same respect and intensity as you treat your work (i.e., your day job).
- Pick activities that align with your goals and your work whenever possible.
- To become an internal Power Player, you can lead an employee resource group (affinity group) or organize a company-sponsored event.
- To become an external Power Player, you can sign up for a prominent role planning or speaking at industry-relevant events.
- To develop yourself as a leader, you can join a not-for-profit board or take on a leadership position in your community.

PAYING IT FORWARD

By establishing yourself as a Power Player, you will be well on your way to achieving your goals. As you create the life you have always dreamed of, make sure that you give back and help the next generation of aspiring professionals. Never forget that you have the power to affect change. No matter your position, whether it's entry-level, mid-level, or more senior, you already have power by virtue of being part of an organization. You are an insider, and your word means something to your organization. Of course, the longer your tenure and the stronger the bonds you develop with your colleagues and management, the more weight your word has at your organization.

One thing anyone can do regardless of his or her tenure concerns job postings. When a position opens at your organization, it may not be widely publicized. Companies tend to recruit in the same few places to fill a position. When you learn about a job opening, you can spread that information to qualified people in your network. Through that simple act, you can help recruit diverse candidates from non-traditional sources. You can also take the next step and help prepare a friend for a job interview at your company. You can explain what HR looks for in job candidates. If you are really impressed with this candidate, you can vouch for him or her by providing a good reference.

INCREASE THE PIPELINE OF DIVERSE CANDIDATES

It is important to be generous to other people and to help diverse junior professionals. One of the ways you can do that is to make sure there is a pipeline of diverse candidates entering your company behind you so your company will become more diverse over time. There are a variety of ways for you to increase the pipeline, and I encourage people to get involved in these activities. You can help by interviewing, recruiting people, or working with HR to broaden the scope of the schools at which they interview. These actions demonstrate your dedication to your organization and the high value you place on diversity and inclusion. If you are one of a few diverse professionals at your organization, you have insights into the culture that prospective diverse hires greatly value. Giving back to diverse junior professionals can also be personally rewarding.

MENTOR/VOUCH FOR JUNIOR EMPLOYEES

You can also be helpful by mentoring diverse professionals behind you. Though it may feel most natural or comfortable to mentor someone who shares an important aspect of your identity, don't feel you have to limit your mentorship in this way. You can also mentor diverse individuals from backgrounds different from your own. One commonality among most new hires is that they won't know the unwritten rules at your company. For these individuals to have a successful start, it is important that somebody explain these unwritten rules to them. You could be that person.

You could also help them within the company by vouching for them, saying positive things about them based on things you have observed or experienced. That kind of information may make people in the majority culture comfortable enough "to take a risk" by working with someone diverse and different from them. Your backing will help that person access better work assignments and development opportunities. Make it clear to the diverse junior professionals that you are helping them and that you expect them to mentor and vouch for the people behind them. Though the person you vouch for may not be able to help you, he or she can certainly pay it forward.

Looking beyond what you can do within your organization, you can also help diverse candidates by connecting them to people in your network who can help them achieve their goals. Even if you can't directly help someone, you might know of someone else who can. Be generous with your time and network. You know your network better than anyone. Make introductions strategically, keeping in mind that all favors should be repaid.

A former mayor of Chicago once said (and I am paraphrasing here), "Don't send me somebody nobody sent." This quote isn't only colorful; it also communicates that it matters *who* is making the introduction or vouching for the person.

Do not feel obligated to make an introduction if you feel it would be unwise or reflect poorly on your reputation. If you don't feel comfortable doing something, you shouldn't do it. Say, for example, a diverse candidate comes to you with a request but has a history of inconsistent performance. Be careful how you turn down the request. The world is very small, and the things that you say can come back around to you. You don't owe people an explanation about why you don't want to do something. If you choose to provide an explanation, just know that it can become public. While striving for neutrality, you may unintentionally find yourself in a sea of drama.

CHANNEL YOUR COMPANY'S RESOURCES

Many organizations engage in socially minded activities such as charitable giving and community-service days. These socially responsible activities bring the organization good publicity and can serve as team-building exercises. Channeling your organization's resources toward socially responsible causes you care about is one way to utilize your Power Player status to pay it forward. The most straightforward method is to get your company to financially sponsor a not-for-profit cause about which you are passionate. By getting your company to become a recurring donor, you create a lasting relationship between your company and the not-for-profit organization.

A lot of organizations also have team-building days on which their employees volunteer on a community-service project. Many times, the organizations are looking for a reputable not-for-profit organization to partner with and to create a space for their employees to strengthen bonds by pursuing a good cause together. You can use your Power Player status to get your organization to pick a particular not-for-profit for its community team-building days. This is a great example of a win-win opportunity.

Another example of a win-win comes from my sister. Out of college, she worked as a receptionist for a public relations firm. She heard that the company was going to get rid of its old furniture, which was only a few years old, and get new furniture. The company was going to throw the old furniture away. My sister thought of a family friend who ran a shelter for women and children in domestic abuse situations. She called to see if the shelter wanted some beautiful, slightly used furniture. They did. She asked her boss if the firm would like to donate the furniture. The PR company was happy to do so and got a tax deduction. This is a great example of using your connections to help others, regardless of your role in the company.

SEE SOMETHING, SAY SOMETHING

Finally, I want to suggest that you adopt the tagline used in airports and public transportation terminals across the United States, which is "See Something, Say Something." And by that I mean, if you see something that you know is wrong, be willing to speak out about it. Whether that means filing a complaint with your HR department or having a direct conversation with an individual making offensive comments, there are many ways we can make our office culture more inclusive, fair, and equitable. Dr. Martin Luther King Jr., reflecting on the civil rights movement, said, "In the end, we will remember not the words of our enemies but the silence of our friends."[123]

In today's world, it is important to use your position to do something positive. From day one at an organization, you have power by virtue of being an employee. You can choose to respectfully assert as much of that power as you want to change your organization for the better. In addition, never forget that you have power in life simply by existing. Your choices are powerful, and your actions can help shape the world around you. If each of us does his or her part, our collective effort will break down the barriers that separate us and create a better world for all people.

The following are a set of operational strategies for giving back to help diverse professionals behind you and addressing causes that are important to you.

OPERATIONAL STRATEGIES: PAYING IT FORWARD

- Make sure there are diverse people behind you who will follow your path at the company.
- Help with your organization's recruiting, interviewing, and hiring processes.
- Work with your HR department to expand the channels used to post job openings.
- Mentor diverse professionals behind you. Vouch for any diverse professionals you believe show promise by saying good things about them to your coworkers.
- Direct your company's financial and manpower resources to causes you care about.
- Be willing to harness your network to support a cause you care about.
- "See Something, Say Something."
- Make sure you are doing something each day or each week to make the world a better place. Your legacy matters.

CONCLUSION

We all have the capacity to leave the world better than we found it. For some that will entail making their organizations or industries better along some measure, such as inclusiveness. For others, it will mean advocating for a meaningful cause outside of work. No matter how you decide to pay it forward, one thing is certain—your impact will be greatly increased if you establish yourself as a Power Player

Rule 10

MAINTAIN CAREER FLEXIBILITY

Stay ahead of the curve by maintaining career flexibility and revising your plan as necessary.

The ability to recognize opportunities and move in new—and sometimes unexpected—directions will benefit you no matter your interests or aspirations.

—DREW GILPIN FAUST

No matter how well you play the game, you will not be immune to adverse events over the course of your career. A merger at your company could undo years of progress, and a shakeup in leadership could start you back at square one. You may be working in a hostile environment due to sexual harassment or racism or both. To succeed in these uncertain times, you must be alert to signs of trouble on the horizon. If you have been thinking strategically and objectively about your career and reading the organizational cues, you will be able to stay ahead of the curve. By that I mean you will be able to recognize when troubling times are beginning to develop for you and proactively take the appropriate action to defuse the situation. Whenever possible, you want to be several moves ahead of any negative external event. Although we may never be fully prepared for every possible negative event, there are some steps we can take to build flexibility into our careers to absorb the shocks along the way.

EXECUTIVE SEARCH FIRMS

Executive search firms generally work for an organization on retainer. Since they are retained by the organization, they don't explicitly work for you. However, you are talent they may want to place in response to another organization's search. Always talk to executive search firms and recruiters when they call—even if you aren't interested in moving. Also, be willing to assist them in finding the right person for a job. If you are polite and open to possibilities that come your way, recruiters are more likely to bring you new job opportunities in the future. This allows you to stay informed about what opportunities are out there on the market. By developing a solid relationship with the search firms, when you do want to leave, they will think highly of you and be more likely to work with you. If you are happy with your current position, simply utilize search firms as another source of information and a way to build your network. Helping a friend or a client find a perfect job builds tremendous loyalty and strengthens your bonds with that person. If you ever spot trouble on the horizon, you will have powerful relationships to leverage—both the recruiter you assisted and the friend who got the job.

LINKEDIN/SOCIAL MEDIA IMAGE

These days, LinkedIn is becoming a very useful database that recruiters access to identify potential job candidates. Make sure you keep your career information updated on LinkedIn. Similarly, be very aware of your social media image. Facebook and other posting sites can be accessed by people who may be doing research on you, particularly HR departments of potential employers. Make sure your social media accounts are free of any posts that could make you look bad and hurt your ability to get a job. This means that every single photo matters. Sometimes friends may take photos of you that are not professional and post them on Facebook. It is better for you to see them and get them taken down than for a current or future employer to see them.

Of course, there are a lot of different privacy settings on these sites. Many people aren't fully informed how to use the privacy settings of the various social media platforms. As a result, many people may not have the proper privacy settings on their accounts. As a general rule of thumb, if your posts are not private, they need to be professional. It's important to keep in mind that even though you may tightly manage your privacy settings or public posts, other people within your network may tag you in photos that you find unprofessional, and you have no control over their privacy settings. Therefore, keep your professional reputation in mind when you are in social situations and people begin to take photos. By keeping your image clean, you maximize flexibility in your career.

RÉSUMÉ BOX VS. BASKET OF SKILLS

When looking to make a job or career change, many people look at their past experiences as a guide for suitable employment opportunities. Although the past can inform the future, it should not limit you in any way. For example, your resume summarizes your past work experiences. The longer you have been working in one industry, the more likely it is that you may see yourself only in that industry, and others may see you only in that industry as well. You could open up your career possibilities by viewing your resume as an indicator of the skills you have developed over time as opposed to a box that you must fit into. You need to think about everything you can possibly do with those skills.

If you were looking to change jobs, what would you do? Many people limit themselves to a narrow scope of opportunities within the field that is familiar to them, like going to a different company where they do the exact same work. Far fewer even consider the possibility of shifting to a new industry that needs their skills. Although change can be scary because of uncertain outcomes, moments of change allow us some of the greatest opportunities for reflection.

After several years as a federal prosecutor doing criminal law, I wanted to return to a civil practice. This required me to look at my criminal law skill set and convert it to skills that could be valued in a civil legal practice. Writing skills are valuable everywhere, regardless of the work. Similarly, public speaking skills are highly valued. Be willing to think outside the box as you think about your skills and build your basket of skills.

By staying informed about job opportunities, keeping a clean image, and shifting perspective on how you can apply your skills, you increase career flexibility. These three actions will make it just a little bit easier to weather the tough times.

THREE TOUGH TIMES

Part of hoping for the best and preparing for the worst is running through hypothetical negative scenarios. This chapter will directly address three such negative scenarios: a bad performance review, the departure of your sponsor, and a hostile environment in which you are being sexually harassed.

What happens if you have a bad performance review or make a big mistake?

It can be very hard to recover from a significant mistake that tarnishes your reputation. It is often easier to move to another organization laterally and start fresh than it is to recover from a very bad performance review or a very big mistake. The toughest part about taking a hit to your reputation is that people are often less willing to work with you.

Everyone wants a winner on his or her team, and you just experienced a loss. In order to bounce back, you will need to accept responsibility for your role in the mistake and demonstrate that you have learned from it by changing your behavior appropriately. The ultimate goal is to show that you can be trusted with equally important matters moving forward.[124]

If you choose to stay, you need to see if you can find someone who is in a position of power and influence who is willing to give you another chance. One way to rehabilitate your reputation is to work with that person and do an outstanding job. If that person thinks you did a great job and vouches for you, then your career has a good chance of recovering. Securing one win at a time is the best way to rebuild your reputation. If you don't have a powerful contact like that within your current organization, the best advice is probably to move laterally. My experience for people of color is that most people move up or advance by moving out. It is sometimes easier to secure a promotion when you change jobs than it is to wait your turn at your current organization.

If your sponsor leaves the firm, where will that leave you?

If your sponsor leaves your firm, you need to see if you can move with him or her. Sponsors are hard to come by. If you have developed a valuable relationship with your sponsor, then you may be able to move to the new organization where he or she will continue looking out for you. There are many stories of people who have advanced by following behind their sponsors. Sometimes high-level executives have clauses in their contracts that prevent them from recruiting their former colleagues after they leave. Therefore, your sponsor may not be able to recruit you, but you may be able to leave voluntarily. Sometimes, you might have to wait until the time specified in the contract expires and your sponsor can recruit you.

It's also possible that you don't want to move with your sponsor. In this case, you can turn your sponsor into a mentor and continue to maintain that relationship in its new form moving forward. The good news is that you have found a way to maintain a valuable relationship. The bad news is that you have one fewer person at your organization advocating for you. If you followed the 2 + 1 Rule discussed in "Rule 5: Recruit Mentors and Sponsors" and developed multiple sponsor relationships, then you will still have strong advocates you can rely on. Whether or not you followed the 2 + 1 Rule, it is time to start searching for a new sponsor.

One great starting point is to ask your former sponsor to make introductions to other senior-level executives in your organization who could be your next sponsor. Having your former sponsor vouch for you may make it easier to identify and develop a relationship with a new sponsor. If that doesn't pan out or is not an option, start building a sponsor relationship from scratch. You have done it before, so you can do it again.

What do you do if your work environment is hostile due to sexual harassment or overt racism?

At some point in your career, you may experience a workplace culture that is hostile to you because of sexual harassment or overt racism. You have internal options—you can report it to the Human Resources (HR) Department or to someone in senior management. The HR Department has the obligation to investigate your claim and come up with a resolution. Potential resolutions, assuming your claim is substantiated by the HR Department, include disciplinary action against the perpetrator(s) up to termination. You may want to move to a different department, section, or team. You may want to pursue legal options. You may choose to leave the company. One thing you should not choose to do is stay and continue to be a victim of this hostile work environment. Staying is likely to have a long-term negative impact on your psyche, self-confidence, and self-esteem. You never want to give someone that type of power over you. Maintaining career flexibility gives you the option of moving to a more inclusive workplace environment where you can thrive.

LIFE-CHANGING EVENTS

Above are just three examples of the negative events that could affect your career. There are many others that we didn't discuss that could alter your plans. For example, your company could be acquired, merge with a competitor, or go bankrupt, leading to large layoffs. We could spend all day running through possible scenarios, but we'd rather not go down that rabbit hole. The takeaway is that you should be prepared for possible negative events and always be on the lookout for early warning signs of trouble ahead. If you can read the writing on the wall long before it becomes a reality, you will be in the best position to maneuver to safer ground.

So far, we have only talked about negative events, but there are many positive events that are life changing. Your partner could land a dream job in a new city. Or you could be getting ready to add a child to the family. Both these events surely come with a mixed bag of emotions and do not fit the label of negative events. In these instances, you may voluntarily decide to leave your current position or reduce your hours to accommodate the change in personal circumstances.

Finally, we should not rule out the possibility that you may wake up one day and realize that you want a change of scenery. Even when circumstances haven't changed and there are no bad omens signaling impending danger, you may decide to pursue a different job because your current position isn't right for you. Just like you don't stay with an external activity that doesn't align with your values or goals, you don't want to stay with a company or in a job that really doesn't align with your values or goals for very long. Be willing to change course in order to follow a career path that is more aligned with your goals and provides you a sense of fulfillment.

I had moved to Los Angeles from Chicago to pursue a lifelong dream of living in a warm climate. After six years living in Los Angeles, with the earthquakes, fires, and riots, I began to miss my Chicago life and friends. So I used the move back to Chicago as an opportunity to change my work setting from a law firm to an in-house legal job in a corporation. At the time I made that move, it seemed right for me.

After six years in that corporate legal job, I decided that the commute was too long and that my opportunities for advancement were limited, so I moved to a different corporate legal job eight blocks from my home. That solved the long commute problem, and I hoped it would solve the advancement opportunities issue, too.

In the event you decide to leave an organization, always try to leave on good terms because your reputation will follow you. I always wanted people at the job I was leaving to be sad that I was leaving, so I worked hard through the last day. During exit interviews provide candid feedback, but don't vent or burn any bridges. It is better to leave the door open in case you choose to return than to definitively slam it shut on your way out. You never know when you will cross paths again with someone from your organization. Try to make any separation from your organization a win for both sides. Seek the advice of mentors regarding the timing of your move and the next step for you. Access your network to assist you in the move. Remember, there is nothing shameful in moving to another opportunity. Just think of the move as expanding your network.

The following are operational strategies for preparing yourself for life's unpredictable curveballs.

OPERATIONAL STRATEGIES: MAINTAINING CAREER FLEXIBILITY

- Look for patterns in signals from senior leadership about good times and bad times ahead. Trust your intuition and prepare for trouble ahead when you feel something is off.
- Stay tuned to your internal network, particularly people "in the know," to stay up to date on changes that may be in process.

- Develop relationships with executive search firms and recruiters. Be polite even if you are not interested at the moment. You never know when the connection might come in handy.
- Keep your career information updated on LinkedIn. For all other social media accounts, make sure you maintain a professional image and learn about the privacy setting options.
- Shift perspective to view your experiences as a basket of skills. Think creatively about how you can use your skills in work you find fulfilling and enjoyable. Be willing to think outside the box.
- Always try to leave on good terms to maintain your positive reputation. Don't burn bridges on your way out.

CONCLUSION AND REVISING YOUR PLAN

No matter what the reasoning is, there are a variety of events in life that can be game changers. They serve as natural inflection points for you. There are many questions likely to come up. What should you do now? What is your next move? How easy will it be for you to make that next move? Where do you want to live? What pace do you want for work/life?

Take the time to reflect on the plan you outlined in "Rule 1: Success Is Intentional." Has your definition of success changed? If so, update your definition and your plan. I highly recommend keeping a journal to reflect on your day-to-day experiences as well as to look back and see how far you've come. Life moves so quickly that the brain simply records events as they transpire. Periods of quiet reflection are essential to properly process these events and glean valuable lessons from them.[125] Carve out time to reflect on what you want, why you want it, and how you think you can achieve it.

Now that you know the rules, I sincerely hope you get everything you want out of life. Take time to enjoy life every step of the way.

CONCLUSION

As you set out on your career path, it is important to recognize the realities of your workplace culture. In a wide variety of industries, there is a dominant workplace culture created by White males. Many aspects of that culture have long been used to eliminate people who are different—and they still are. Enormous efforts are being made to change that culture, but the unfortunate aspects of that reality still exist. In my diversity consulting work, I strive to make organizations more diverse and inclusive. Positive change is happening, but at times it can be slow and difficult to perceive. When I think about all the diverse professionals entering the office each day on an uneven playing field, I realize that change cannot come soon enough.

While we continue to make workplace cultures more inclusive, I felt the strong need to disseminate information on how diverse professionals can thrive in their current environments. Knowledge of the unwritten rules of the game will provide a strong foundation for pursuing your aspirations. But it is important to note that there is no substitute for hard work.

By sharing this information with you, I hope to level the playing field to give you a fairer shot at shaping your future. However, no one can eliminate obstacles from your path or do your work for you. Continue to work hard each and every day, but also focus on the other areas that matter: networking, mentors and sponsors, professional appearance, and self-promotion, among others. You must own your success and drive forward to achieve your vision of it. No one else will do it for you.

There may be some people who don't like these rules or don't agree with them for whatever reason. Others may recognize that these rules are in operation at their organization but refuse to play the game on the grounds that it perpetuates the dominant culture. To them I say that everything in life is a choice. I felt a sense of duty to share the information I wish I had known when I started my career. I wholeheartedly believe that the dominant culture needs to adapt to become more inclusive. That is why I work day in and day out to shape better workplace cultures. I believe you have to do everything you can to simultaneously function within the current culture and work to improve it. The best way to change the culture is to get into a position of power and influence.

But the challenge is that you may work in a place where these rules are in effect. If you don't play the game well, you may not get to a position in which you can make the organization better for those who follow you. If you don't want to play the game, that is OK. If you encounter a workplace culture that doesn't match your values, you can choose to go somewhere else. Make a conscious decision to say to yourself, "I know what the rules are, and I don't want to play this game." In that situation, you are in control. You intentionally choose to leave. That's fine.

I wrote this book for the diverse professionals who are trying to succeed at their organizations and have the funny feeling that they are in the dark. These diverse professionals don't know about these unwritten rules or how to effectively act in accordance with them. These hardworking, intelligent professionals get passed over for promotions and overlooked for high-profile work assignments and just don't know why. With insider knowledge of some areas they may have been overlooking, these diverse professionals can be more strategic and less reactive in their careers.

If you decide to play the game, I want you to be in a position to play it better than anyone else. I want you to rise to leadership roles and to create a more diverse and inclusive workplace where the rules are multicultural and equitable. I wish you much professional success.

FULL LIST OF OPERATIONAL STRATEGIES

RULE 1: SUCCESS IS INTENTIONAL

Operational Strategies: Visualizing Success

- Form a clear vision of your dream life as far out as possible (5, 10, even 20 years).
- Think about your personal and professional lives when envisioning your future.

Operational Strategies: Making a Plan

- Write your goals down in as much detail as possible.
- Work backward from your end goal to identify concrete steps to your destination.
- Set S.M.A.R.T.E.R. goals to reach each stepping-stone on your path.
- Reflect on your progress frequently, and adjust your plan of action as necessary.
- Recruit trusted advisers to call you out when you stray from your path.
- Use goal-setting platforms, like the app STICKK, that help track your progress.

RULE 2: MASTER THE PSYCHOLOGICAL GAME

Operational Strategies: Your Psychological Game

- Stay in touch with other high-performing diverse people.
- Don't take things personally.
- Zoom out and remember your vision.

Operational Strategies: Effective Communication

- Golden Rule: say what you mean and mean what you say.
- Get to the point. Eliminate unnecessary details and qualifiers.
- Read the news and industry-relevant publications to stay informed.

Operational Strategies: Receiving Criticism

- Resist the urge to be defensive.
- Ask clarifying questions.
- Ask for concrete examples of abstract feedback.
- Take time to process feedback before pursuing next steps.

RULE 3: THE NUMBERS MATTER

Operational Strategies: Reducing Errors

- Read e-mails and other written content out loud.
- Double- and triple-check your work.
- If you make a mistake, correct it and devise ways to prevent similar mistakes.
- Check in informally to ensure you are taking the right approach on an assignment.

Operational Strategies: Understanding the Metrics

- Identify the key metrics on your organization's performance evaluation form.
- Ask reliable sources what types of experiences count in each category.

- Get your review "translated" by a mentor or veteran who works at the company.
- Catalogue how your successes fulfill the organization's goals and key metrics.

Operational Strategies: Peer Comparison

- Figure out how you compare to your peers.
- Keep up to date on changes in your peer group and the metrics that matter.

RULE 4: ACTIVELY NETWORK

Operational Strategies: Staying in Touch

- Strive to form a meaningful connection.
- Include a personal touch in each message.
- Follow-up messages should be concise and timely.
- Follow up to thank the person who put you in touch with a new contact.
- Use mealtimes to catch up with an office friend or get to know a new contact.
- Host an event to maximize your time and catch up with many people in one place.

Operational Strategies: Building Your Network

- Network across lines of difference (e.g., racial, ethnic, gender, etc.).
- Develop relationships with "go-to" people long before you need to ask for a favor.
- Treat office administrative staff and your peers with respect.

- Be nice to gatekeepers (i.e., secretaries and assistants).
- "See and be seen" at company networking events by arriving early.
- Be willing to sit with the boss.

Operational Strategies: Thoughtfully Making Connections

- Do your research and look up the people you may meet at an event.
- Build a supportive personal network separate from your professional network.

Operational Strategies: Asking for Favors

- Whenever you request a favor, ask what you can do in return.
- Keep a mental account of favors received and favors granted.
- Be willing to give generously within your means. You will reap the rewards later.

Operational Strategies: Leveraging Your Network

- Build your network before you need to access it for a favor.
- Deepen relationships with people you already know and meet their contacts.

Operational Strategies: Reducing Isolation

- Stay connected to other diverse people through affinity groups or associations.
- Build professional relationships through your outside-work activities.

Operational Strategies: Givers, Takers, and Matchers

- Identify the people in your network as Givers, Takers, or Matchers.
- Align yourself with Givers and Matchers.
- Weed out the Takers who may try to take advantage of you.

RULE 5: RECRUIT MENTORS AND SPONSORS

Operational Strategies: Building Your Mentor Team

- Identify at least two mentors within your organization.
- Identify at least two mentors outside your organization.
- Make sure you have a diverse set of mentors across lines of difference.

Operational Strategies: Building Your Sponsor Team

- Be mindful of how your words, wardrobe, and behavior will be perceived.
- Be professional. Avoid flirting and wearing revealing cocktail attire.
- Meet in a public space in or around your office.
- Avoid settings that can be construed as romantic (e.g., dimly lit restaurants).
- Carefully consider the time when scheduling a catch-up session.
- Schedule breakfast meetings at the office or at a nearby restaurant.
- Schedule meetings in the office after work around 5:30 or 6:00 p.m.—but not too late.
- Ask a sponsor out to drinks or a meal in a group setting.
- Signal that your personal needs are met.
- Get to know your sponsor's family/significant other.

- Whenever appropriate, invite your family or significant other to join a meeting.
- Avoid awkward situations (e.g., renting a cabin as a team-bonding event).
- Participate in your company's formal mentoring or sponsorship program.

Operational Strategies: Recruiting Mentors

- Identify your short-term (1-2 years) and long-term (5,10,15 years) goals.
- Share your goals with potential mentors and gauge the feedback to determine fit.
- Ask prospective mentors about their life stories.

Operational Strategies: Recruiting Sponsors

- Do a diagnostic assessment of your skills to identify strengths and weaknesses.
- Be ready and willing to articulate the mutual benefits to a potential sponsor.
- Identify potential sponsors and initiate professional interactions with them.

Operational Strategies: Nurturing Relationships

- Ask for help when you need it.
- Be strategic about to whom you say yes. Always say "yes" to your sponsor.

- Propose solutions rather than presenting excuses after saying yes to a request.
- Be open to constructive criticism. Don't get defensive; get reflective.

Operational Strategies: Being a Good Mentee/Protégé

- Develop relationships with key people before you need to ask for anything.
- Look for opportunities to give something back to mentors and sponsors.
- Be willing to mentor others to pay it forward.
- Maintain the confidentiality of things your mentor or sponsor tells you.

RULE 6: INVEST IN YOUR PROFESSIONAL APPEARANCE

Operational Strategies: When in Doubt, Hold That Thought

- Think carefully before getting a piercing or a tattoo in a highly visible place.
- Ask around to determine what is appropriate attire for different company events.

Operational Strategies: Be Client Ready

- After getting dressed, ask yourself if you would feel comfortable meeting a client.
- Look to the senior management for a guide on how you should dress.

Operational Strategies: Invest in Your Appearance

- Adhere to the company dress code with a little tweak up.
- Invest in a few outfits each year that are professional and make you feel good.

Operational Strategies: Colors Matter

- Be mindful of the color(s) you choose for your hair, nails, and makeup.
- Inventory your work clothes, checking for appropriateness of the color, fit, and style.
- Develop a relationship with a personal shopper who can help you choose clothing.

Operational Strategies: Address Accents

- Consider seeing a speech therapist and look into accent reduction training.
- Get a voice coach who can help you work on communication.

RULE 7: STRATEGICALLY SELF-PROMOTE

Operational Strategies: Building Your Brand

- Think of three adjectives or traits you would want others to use to describe you.
- Create a concrete vision for your personal brand.

Operational Strategies: Information Gathering

- Ask reliable sources about how people perceive you in the office.
- Find ways to incorporate highly-valued traits into your brand.

Eleven Operational Strategies for Self-Promotion

1. Secure Your Insecurities.
2. Keep a Folder of Accomplishments.
3. Accept Compliments Graciously.
4. Receive Credit for Your Work.
5. Loop in Your Boss.
6. Participate in Company Events.
7. Form Self-Promotion Partnerships.
8. Elevate Your Small Talk.
9. Know Your Audience.
10. Say No… Because.
11. Create a Bio, Résumé, and Social Media Profile That Speak for You.

RULE 8: BE MINDFUL OF WORK-LIFE INTEGRATION

Operational Strategies: At Work—Physical Well-Being Tips

- Take a lap around your office every hour to stretch your legs and rest your eyes.
- Get a watch or app that reminds you to move around and stay active all day.

- Take a flight of stairs instead of the elevator or escalator.
- Keep healthy snacks in your bag or desk.
- Drink water throughout the day to stay hydrated.

Operational Strategies: At Work—Mental Well-Being Tips

- Find ways to incorporate your interests into work events.
- If possible, work remotely to shake up your routine and get a change of scenery.
- Be mindful about balancing "me time" and "face time."
- Go out for lunch with a friend or to network.
- Take a walk or two around the block to clear your head.
- Schedule fun events during the week that you look forward to doing after work.
- When traveling for business, try to reach out to friends at your destination.
- Stay at the same hotel when traveling to the same city often so the staff can get to know you and take better care of you.
- Consider staying over the weekend to catch up with friends or do some sightseeing.
- Explore a new restaurant or local attraction with your coworkers.
- Avoid traveling with colleagues who stress you out.

Operational Strategies: Away from Work—Physical Well-Being Tips
Exercise Tips

- Invest in nice workout clothes and gym shoes that make you feel good.
- Work out first thing in the morning for a mood and energy boost.

Sleep Tips

- Maintain a consistent sleep schedule.
- Allow your mind to slowly wind down by dimming the lights and putting away electronic screens an hour before heading to bed.
- Don't let your phone wake you up throughout the night with e-mail and news alerts.
- Sleep in cool temperatures because your body naturally cools down at night.

Operational Strategies: Away from Work—Mental Well-Being Strategies

- Block off time in your schedule for a walk through a park or other natural space.
- Stay in touch with people who share key attributes of your identity.
- Consider joining a professional association or a cause that is important to you.
- Connect with family or good friends.
- Schedule a weekly massage.
- Pamper yourself in ways that fit your budget on a routine basis.
- Try acupuncture to keep your chi flowing.

Operational Strategies: Buy Time

- Pay people to do things you don't want to do, like to do, or need to do.
- Hire a cleaning service to clean your living space twice a month or more often.

- Hire individuals who can organize your files and paperwork for you.
- Try a grocery delivery or meal delivery service.
- If you have kids, be sure to put a baby sitter on retainer on the weekends.
- Make the most of your exercise time—get a personal trainer.

RULE 9: BECOME A POWER PLAYER AND PAY IT FORWARD

Operational Strategies: Being a Power Player

- Look to find whatever your job lacks through activities outside of work.
- Treat external commitments with the same respect as you treat your day job.
- Pick activities that align with your goals and your work whenever possible.
- Lead an employee resource group or organize company-sponsored events.
- Take on a prominent role planning or speaking at industry-relevant events.
- Look for leadership opportunities in your external activities and community.

Operational Strategies: Paying It Forward

- Make sure there are diverse people behind you at your organization.
- Participate in your organization's recruiting, interviewing, and hiring processes.

- Help your HR department expand the channels used to post job openings.
- Mentor and vouch for diverse professionals behind you.
- Direct your company's resources to causes you care about.
- Be willing to harness your network to support a cause you care about.
- "See Something, Say Something."
- Do something each day or each week to make the world a better place.

RULE 10: MAINTAIN CAREER FLEXIBILITY

Operational Strategies: Maintaining Career Flexibility

- Trust your intuition and prepare for trouble ahead when you feel something is off.
- Befriend people "in the know" to stay informed on upcoming changes.
- Develop relationships with executive search firms and recruiters.
- Maintain a professional image on social media and use the privacy settings.
- Think creatively and view your experiences as a basket of skills.
- Leave on good terms to maintain your positive reputation.

ACKNOWLEDGEMENT

It is said that it takes a village to raise a child and that same expression is applicable to the writing of this book. It represents the contributions of my village. I have been inspired by the many women and men I have worked with through the years who have shared their experiences with me and the challenges they have faced and overcome. Most importantly in my village would be my mother, Lillian, who has been a role model, mentor, and supporter to me. I thank her for traveling this life with me and teaching me her life lessons. I am inspired as well by my niece, Liz and my nephews, Raymond, Jaxon, and Xavier. They make me want the world to be a better place and I leave this book so that by the time they are adults, it will be a much more diverse and inclusive world.

I thank my co-author, Sudheer Poluru, a key member of my village. Sudheer was my sounding board, and my partner in getting these presentations into writing. I could not have done it without him and he made the book better for his contributions. He was a pleasure to work with and captured my voice and approach well. I thank India Peek Jensen for her discerning feedback on drafts and at every stage of the book writing and editing process. Another important village member is Sandra Yamate. Sandra reviewed early editions of the book and provided much needed constructive criticism as well as support. She has been a life-long supporter, inspiration, and good friend. I am also grateful for the time and feedback provided by Bridgette J. Slater and Kavya Poluru, two women beginning their professional careers. Their insights were extremely helpful and were incorporated in revisions to the book. This book was made better by the editorial assistance of Jenny Chandler and the beautiful designs of Grace Han. I will be forever grateful to them.

My village contains the support of my stepmother, Elizabeth, sister, Ruthie, sister-in-law, Natalie, and my brothers, Claudius and Michael. I have learned from them and included some of their lessons in this book. I stand on the shoulders of my grandparents in writing this book. They didn't have the opportunities I have had despite their intelligence and courage, but they shared with me their stories and spirit. I will always be grateful for their eternal support.

I also want to thank Team Sharon, Kurt Hill, Tara Sullivan, Amie Shimmel, Sara Davenport, Jason Raynor, and Donita Nurse, the people who have kept me together through all the challenges in my professional life. I couldn't have completed this book without you. My sister friends, Tommie, Toni, Aretha, and Tonik deserve to be mentioned. They form my network for support and have served in that role since college. I thank them for always being there.

Finally, I want to thank the thousands of people who listened to earlier versions of presentations on this topic and asked questions and shared their experiences. I listened to you and your feedback helped to make this book much better. Now I hope each of us works to make the world a more diverse and inclusive place.

NOTES

The Playing Field

1. U.S. Census Bureau, "Quick Facts," accessed January 4, 2018, https://www.census.gov/quickfacts/fact/table/US/SEX255216.

2. Claire Zillman, "How Ruth Bader Ginsburg Called Out a Man's Unconscious Bias Against Her," *Fortune*, September 29, 2017, accessed January 4, 2018, http://fortune.com/2017/09/29/ruth-bader-ginsburg-supreme-court-discrimination/.

3. Bureau of Labor Statistics, "Labor Force Statistics from the Current Population Survey," accessed January 4, 2018, https://www.bls.gov/cps/cpsaat11.htm.

4. National Association for Law Placement, Inc., "2017 Report on Diversity in U.S. Law Firms," accessed January 4, 2018, https://www.nalp.org/uploads/2017NALPReportonDiversityinUSLawFirms.pdf; U.S. Census Bureau, "Quick Facts." (Percentages for males calculated using the formula 100% - % female = % male.)

5. Ibid. (Percentages for White associates and partners calculated using the formula 100% - total percentage minority from tables 5 and 6 of the NALP 2017 Report on Diversity.)

6. *Diversity & The Bar*, "MCCA'S Eighteenth Annual General Counsel Survey," accessed January 4, 2018, http://www.diversityandthebardigital.com/datb/winter_2017/MobilePagedReplica.action?pm=2&folio=8#pg8.

7. Valentina Zarya, "Why There Are No Black Women Running Fortune 500 Companies," *Fortune*, January 16, 2017, accessed January 4, 2018, http://fortune.com/2017/01/16/black-women-fortune-500/.

8. Danielle Wiener-Bronner, "Soon, There Will Be Just Three Black Fortune 500 CEOs," *CNN Money*, October 20, 2017, accessed January 4, 2018, http://money.cnn.com/2017/10/19/news/companies/black-ceos-fortune-500/index.html.

9. Issuu, Inc., HACR 2013 Corporate Governance Appendix, last modified August 3, 2014, accessed January 4, 2018, https://issuu.com/hacr/docs/2013_hacr_cgs-appendix.

10. Jose Marquez, "Congratulations to the First Latina CEO of a Fortune 500: Geisha Williams, PG&E," *Tech Latino*, November 18, 2016, accessed January 4, 2018, http://techlatino.org/2016/11/congratulations-to-the-first-latina-ceo-of-a-fortune-500-geisha-williams-pge/.

11. Diversity Best Practices, "Five Asian CEOs to Know," last modified May 1, 2017, accessed January 4, 2018, http://www.diversitybestpractices.com/5-asian-ceos-to-know.

12. Jonathan Vanian, "HPE CEO Meg Whitman to Step Down," *Fortune*, November 21, 2017, accessed January 4, 2018, http://fortune.com/2017/11/21/meg-whitman-step-down-hewlett-packard-enterprise-ceo.

13. Reuters Staff, "Anthem Top Executive Swedish to Become Adviser, Boudreaux Named CEO," *Reuters*, November 6, 2017, accessed January 4, 2018, https://www.reuters.com/article/us-anthem-ceo/anthem-top-executive-swedish-to-become-adviser-boudreaux-named-ceo-idUSKBN1D619C.

14. Fortune Editors, "These Are the Women CEOs Leading Fortune 500 Companies," *Fortune*, June 7, 2017, accessed January 4, 2018, http://fortune.com/2017/06/07/fortune-500-women-ceos/.

15. Deloitte, "Missing Pieces Report: The 2016 Board Diversity Census of Women and Minorities on Fortune 500 Boards," accessed January 4, 2018, https://www2.deloitte.com/us/en/pages/center-for-board-effectiveness/articles/board-diversity-census-missing-pieces.html.

16. Ibid.

17. Ibid; U.S. Census Bureau, "Quick Facts."

18. "Board Diversity at an Impasse?" *Heidrick & Struggles CEO & Board Practice*, accessed January 4, 2018, http://www.heidrick.com/-/media/Publications%20and%20Reports/Board_Monitor_Board_diversity_at_an_impasse.pdf.

19. Ibid.

20. Vivian Hunt, Dennis Layton, and Sara Prince, "Why Diversity Matters," McKinsey & Company, January 2015, accessed January 4, 2018, http://www.mckinsey.com/business-functions/organization/our-insights/why-diversity- matters.

21. Vivian Hunt, Sara Prince, Sundiatu Dixon-Fyle, and Lareina Yee, "Delivering through Diversity," McKinsey & Company, January 2018, accessed January 22, 2018, https://www.mckinsey.com/business-functions/organization/our-insights/delivering-through-diversity

22. "Board Diversity at an Impasse?" *Heidrick & Struggles CEO & Board Practice*.

23. DataUSA, "Physicians & Surgeons," accessed January 4, 2018, https://datausa.io/profile/soc/291060/#demographics.

24. Association of American Medical Colleges, "Table A-12: Applicants, First-Time Applicants, Acceptees, and Matriculants to U.S. Medical Schools by Race/Ethnicity, 2014–2015 through 2017–2018," accessed January 4, 2018, https://www.aamc.org/download/321480/data/factstablea12.pdf; Bureau of Labor Statistics, "Labor Force Statistics from the Current Population Survey"; US Census Bureau, "Quick Facts." (Percentages for males calculated using the formula 100% - % female = % male.)

25. Ibid. (Percentage for White physicians/surgeons was calculated using the formula 100% - racial and ethnic minority group percentages [Asian, Black/African American, and Hispanic percentages from the Association of American Medical Colleges Table A-12]. Also, medical school student columns add up to 86.2 percent because the numbers for the mixed race, other, and not reported categories are not shown.)

26. Kate Conger, "Exclusive: Here's the Full 10-Page Anti-Diversity Screed Circulating Internally at Google [Updated]," *Gizmodo*, August 5, 2017, accessed January 4, 2018, https://gizmodo.com/exclusive-heres-the-full-10-page-anti-diversity-screed- 1797564320.

27. Dana Varinsky, "Science Totally Debunks That Shocking Manifesto That Got a Google Employee Fired," Science Alert, August 9, 2017, originally published in *Business Insider*, accessed January 4, 2018, https://www.sciencealert.com/a-google-employee-was-fired-after-blaming-biology-for-tech-s-gender-gap-but-the-science-shows-he-s-wrong.

28. Sheryl Estrada, "Apple's Head of Diversity Apologizes for Saying '12 White, Blue-Eyed Blond Men in a Room' Are Diverse," *DiversityInc*, October 17, 2017, accessed January 4, 2018, http://www.diversityinc.com/news/apples-head-diversity-apologizes-saying-12-white-blue-eyed-blond-men-room-diverse/.

29. Dan Primack, "Wall Street Outpaces Silicon Valley on Gender Equality," *Axios*, August 8, 2017, accessed January 4, 2018, https://www.axios.com/wall-street-outpaces-silicon-valley-on-gender-equality-2470698125.html.

30. Apple, "Inclusion & Diversity," accessed January 4, 2018, https://www.apple.com/diversity/; Microsoft, "Global Diversity and Inclusion: Our Workforce," accessed January 4, 2018, https://www.microsoft.com/en-us/diversity/inside-microsoft/default.aspx#epgDivFocusArea; Google, "Our Workforce Composition," accessed January 4, 2018, https://diversity.google/commitments/; Facebook, "Facebook Diversity Update: Building a More Diverse, Inclusive Workplace" accessed January 4, 2018, https://fbnewsroomus.files.wordpress.com/2017/08/fb_diversity_2017_final.pdf; US Census Bureau, "Quick Facts."

31. Ibid.

32. Ibid.

33. Scott E. Page, *The Difference: How the Power of Diversity Creates Better Groups, Firms, Schools, and Societies* (Princeton, NJ: Princeton University Press, 2007).

34. Hunt, Prince, Dixon-Fyle, and Yee, "Delivering through Diversity."

35. Katherine W. Phillips, "How Diversity Makes Us Smarter," *Scientific American*, October 1, 2014, accessed January 4, 2018, https://www.scientificamerican.com/article/how-diversity-makes-us-smarter/.

36. Catalyst, "Why Diversity Matters," last modified July 2013, accessed January 4, 2018, http://www.catalyst.org/system/files/why_diversity_matters_catalyst_0.pdf.

37. Lone Christiansen, Huidan Lin, Joana Pereira, Petia Topalova, and Rima Turk, "Gender Diversity in Senior Positions and Firm Performance: Evidence from Europe," *International Monetary Fund*, Working Paper 16/50 (2016), accessed January 4, 2018, https://www.imf.org/external/pubs/ft/wp/2016/wp1650.pdf.

38. For a great guide on planning out and visualizing your goals, read *Write It Down, Make It Happen: Knowing What You Want and Getting It* by Henriette Anne Klauser. Dr. Klauser shares easy-to-follow tips and plenty of anecdotes detailing how the first step toward realizing your goals is clarifying your vision on paper.

39. Marianne Bertrand and Sendhil Mullainathan, "Are Emily and Greg More Employable Than Lakisha and Jamal?" *National Bureau of Economic Research,* Working Paper 9873 (2003), accessed January 4, 2018, http://www.nber.org/papers/w9873.pdf.

Rule 1: Success Is Intentional

40. Accenture, "Accenture Research Finds Most Professionals Believe They Can 'Have It All,'" last modified March 1, 2013, accessed January 4, 2018, https://newsroom.accenture.com/subjects/corporate-citizenship-philanthropy/accenture-research-finds-most-professionals-believe-they-can-have-it-all.htm.

41. Nancy Jennings, Suzanne Lovett, Lee Cuba, Joe Swingle, and Heather Lindkvist, "'What Would Make This a Successful Year for You?': How Students Define Success in College," *Liberal Education* 99(2) (2013), accessed January 4, 2018, https://www.aacu.org/publications-research/periodicals/what-would-make-successful-year-you-how-students-define-success.

42. University of Cambridge, "Questioning the Meaning of Success," accessed January 4, 2018, https://www.cam.ac.uk/women-at-cambridge/introduction/questioning-the-meaning-of-success.

43. Jacquelyn Smith, "This Is How Americans Define Success," *Business Insider*, October 3, 2014, accessed January 4, 2018, http://www.businessinsider.com/how-americans-now-define-success-2014-10.

44. Shawn Achor, "The Happy Secret to Better Work," TED.com, May 2011, accessed January 4, 2018, https://www.ted.com/talks/shawn_achor_the_happy_secret_ to_better_work/transcript.

45. To learn more about positive psychology, check out these two books: *The Happiness Advantage*, by Shawn Achor. This book addresses how we can reprogram our brains to be more positive to gain a competitive advantage at work. *Choose the Life You Want: The Mindful Way to Happiness*, by Tal Ben-Shahar. While at Harvard, the author taught positive psychology, frequently cited as the Ivy League institution's most popular course. In his book, Ben-Shahar draws on research to identify many small choices that we make day to day that can have a profound impact on our long-term happiness.

46. Ibid

47. George T. Doran, "There's a S.M.A.R.T. Way to Write Management's Goals and Objectives," *Management Review* 70(11) (1981): 35–6, accessed January 4, 2018, http://community.mis.temple.edu/mis0855002fall2015/files/2015/10/ S.M.A.R.T-Way-Management-Review.pdf.

48. R.L. Adams, "Setting S.M.A.R.T.E.R. Goals: 7 Steps to Achieving Any Goal," *Wanderlust Worker*, accessed January 4, 2018, https://www.wanderlustworker.com/setting-s-m-a-r-t-e-r-goals-7-steps-to-achieving-any-goal/.

49. Edwin A. Locke, Karyll N. Shaw, Lise M. Saari, and Gary P. Latham, *"Goal Setting and Task Performance: 1969–1980," Psychological Bulletin* 90(1) (1981): 125–52, doi: 10.1037/0033-2909.90.1.125.

50. Dominican University of California, "News Room: Study Focuses on Strategies for Achieving Goals, Resolutions," accessed January 4, 2018, https://www.dominican.edu/dominicannews/study-highlights-strategies-for-achieving-goals.

Rule 2: The Psychological Game

51. Claude M. Steele and Joshua Aronson, "Stereotype Threat and the Intellectual Test Performance of African Americans," *Journal of Personality and Social Psychology* 69(5) (1995): 797–811, doi: 10.1037/0022-3514.69.5.797.

52. Patricia M. Gonzales, Hart Blanton, and Kevin J. Williams, "The Effects of Stereotype Threat and Double-Minority Status on the Test Performance of Latino Women," *Personality and Social Psychology Bulletin* 28(5) (2002): 659–70, doi: 10.1177/0146167202288010.

53. Catherine Good, Joshua Aronson, and Jayne A. Harder, "Problems in the Pipeline: Stereotype Threat and Women's Achievement in High-Level Math Courses," *Journal of Applied Developmental Psychology* 29(1) (2008): 17–28, doi: 10.1016/j.appdev.2007.10.004.

54. Study.com, "Self-Fulfilling Prophecies in Psychology: Definition & Examples," accessed January 4, 2018, http://study.com/academy/lesson/self-fulfilling-prophecies-in-psychology-definition-examples.html.

55. Mindset, "What is Mindset?" accessed January 4, 2018, https://mindsetonline.com/whatisit/about/.

56. Adam Grant, "The Surprising Habits of Original Thinkers," TED.com, February 2016, accessed January 4, 2018, https://www.ted.com/talks/adam_grant_the_surprising_habits_of_original_thinkers/transcript.

57. Katty Kay and Claire Shipman, *The Confidence Code: The Science and Art of Self-Assurance—What Women Should Know* (New York: HarperCollins, 2014).

58. Sylvia Ann Hewlett, *Forget a Mentor, Find a Sponsor: The New Way to Fast-Track Your Career* (Boston: Harvard Business Review Press, 2013), 171–2.

59. Tonja Jacobi and Dylan Schweers, "Justice, Interrupted: The Effect of Gender, Ideology and Seniority at Supreme Court Oral Arguments," *Virginia Law Review* 103(7) (2017), accessed January 4, 2018, http://virginialawreview.org/volumes/content/justice-interrupted-effect-gender-ideology-and-seniority- supreme-court-oral.

60. For more strategies on effective communication, read *Nice Girls Still Don't Get the Corner Office: Unconscious Mistakes Women Make That Sabotage Their Careers* by Lois P. Frankel, PhD. Although aimed at women, the tips are helpful for anyone who aspires to get to a leadership role.

61. Hewlett, *Forget a Mentor, Find a Sponsor*, 181.

62. Ibid, 155–7.

Rule 3: The Numbers Matter

63. Pam M. S. Nugent, "Fundamental Attribution Error," *Psychology Dictionary*, May 11, 2013, accessed January 4, 2018, https://psychologydictionary.org/fundamental- attribution-error/.

64. Anders Frederiksen, Fabian Lange, and Ben Kriechel, "Subjective Performance Evaluations and Employee Careers," *Journal of Economic Behavior & Organization* 134 (2017): 408–29, doi: 10.1016/j.jebo.2016.12.016.

65. Malin Malmstrom, Jeaneth Johansson, and Joakim Wincent, "Gender Stereotypes and Venture Support Decisions: How Governmental Venture Capitalists Socially Construct Entrepreneurs' Potential," *Entrepreneurship Theory and Practice* 41(5) (2017): 833–60, doi: 10.1111/etap.12275.

66. Malin Malmstrom, Jeaneth Johansson, and Joakim Wincent, "We Recorded VCs' Conversations and Analyzed How Differently They Talk About Female Entrepreneurs," *Harvard Business Review*, May 17, 2017, accessed January 4, 2018, https://hbr.org/2017/05/we-recorded-vcs-conversations-and-analyzed-how-differently-they-talk-about-female-entrepreneurs.

Rule 4: Actively Network

67. Stephen R. Covey, *The 7 Habits of Highly Effective People: Powerful Lessons in Personal Change* (New York: Simon & Schuster, 2013).

68. Bradley A. Hanson and Thomas W. Harrell, "Predictors of Business Success over Two Decades: An MBA Longitudinal Study," *Organizational Behavior*, Working Paper 788 (1985), accessed January 4, 2018, https://www.gsb.stanford.edu/faculty-research/working-papers/predictors-business-success-over-two-decades-mba-longitudinal-study.

69. Keith Ferrazzi and Tahl Raz, *Never Eat Alone: And Other Secrets to Success, One Relationship at a Time* (New York: Crown Business, 2014), 134.

70. Ibid, 112–3.

71. Neal J. Roese, "Being Too Busy for Friends Won't Help Your Career," *Harvard Business Review*, July 28, 2017, accessed January 4, 2018, https://hbr.org/2017/07/being-too-busy-for-friends-wont-help-your-career.

72. Ferrazzi and Raz, *Never Eat Alone*, 136–7.

73. Emma Seppala and Marissa King, "Burnout at Work Isn't Just About Exhaustion. It's Also About Loneliness," *Harvard Business Review*, June 29, 2017, accessed January 4, 2018, https://hbr.org/2017/06/burnout-at-work-isnt-just-about-exhaustion-its-also-about-loneliness.

74. Roese, "Being Too Busy for Friends Won't Help Your Career."

75. TINYpulse, "7 Vital Trends Disrupting Today's Workplace," accessed January 4, 2018, https://www.tinypulse.com/resources/employee-engagement-survey-2013.

76. Adam Grant, "Are You a Giver or a Taker?" TED.com, November 2016, accessed January 4, 2018, https://www.ted.com/talks/adam_grant_are_you_a_giver_or_a_taker/transcript. For more information, read *Give and Take* by Adam Grant.

Rule 5: Recruit Mentors and Sponsors

77. Hewlett, *Forget a Mentor, Find a Sponsor*, 19–22, 33, 37.

78. Lois Tamir and Laura Finfer, "Younger and Older Executives Need Different Things from Coaching," *Harvard Business Review*, July 6, 2017, accessed January 4, 2018, https://hbr.org/2017/07/younger-and-older-executives-need-different-things-from-coaching.

79. Understanding Prejudice, "The Psychology of Prejudice: An Overview: Ingroup Favoritism," accessed January 4, 2018, http://www.understandingprejudice.org/apa/english/page7.htm.

80. Richard Farnell, "Mentor People Who Aren't Like You," *Harvard Business Review*, April 17, 2017, accessed January 4, 2018, https://hbr.org/2017/04/mentor-people-who-arent-like-you.

81. Dan Schawbel, "Sylvia Ann Hewlett: Find a Sponsor Instead of a Mentor," *Forbes*, September 10, 2013, accessed January 4, 2018, https://www.forbes.com/sites/danschawbel/2013/09/10/sylvia-ann-hewlett-find-a-sponsor-instead-of-a-mentor.

82. Original Cast, "The Room Where It Happens," *Hamilton* soundtrack, Atlantic Records, B01CTFZI32, 2015, album.

83. Hewlett, *Forget a Mentor, Find a Sponsor*, 24, 109–10.

84. Ibid, 13–50.

85. Ibid, 23.

86. Sylvia Ann Hewlett, Kerrie Peraino, Laura Sherbin, and Karen Sumberg, "The Sponsor Effect: Breaking Through the Last Glass Ceiling," *Harvard Business Review Research Report*, (2010), accessed January 4, 2018, https://hbr.org/product/the-sponsor-effect-breaking-through-the-last-glass-ceiling/10428-PDF-ENG.

87. Hewlett, *Forget a Mentor, Find a Sponsor*, 80, 90.

88. Ibid, 75–6.

89. Ibid, 80–1.

90. Claire Cain Miller, "It's Not Just Mike Pence. Americans Are Wary of Being Alone with the Opposite Sex," *New York Times*, July 1, 2017, accessed January 4, 2018, https://www.nytimes.com/2017/07/01/upshot/members-of-the-opposite-sex-at-work-gender-study.html.

91. Hewlett, *Forget a Mentor, Find a Sponsor*, 139–40.

92. Ibid, 115, 131.

93. Carolyn O'Hara, "How to Break Up with Your Mentor," *Harvard Business Review*, May 29, 2014, accessed January 4, 2018, https://hbr.org/2014/05/how-to-break-up-with-your-mentor.

Rule 6: Invest in Your Professional Appearance

94. Claire Zillman, "Congress's 'No Sleeveless' Dress Code Is Another Arbitrary Barrier for Women," *Fortune*, July 7, 2017, accessed January 4, 2018, http://fortune.com/2017/07/07/congress-dress-code/.

95. Hewlett, *Forget a Mentor, Find a Sponsor*, 146.

96. Yuki Noguchi, "Power Suits: How Dressing for Success at Work Can Pay Off," *National Public Radio*, March 18, 2016, accessed January 4, 2018, http://www.npr.org/2016/03/18/469669877/power-suits-how-dressing-for-success-at-work-can-pay-off.

97. Hajo Adam and Adam D. Galinsky, "Enclothed Cognition," *Journal of Experimental Social Psychology* 48(4) (2012): 918–25, doi: 10.1016/j.jesp.2012.02.008.

98. Mark Barber, "New Index Puts Social Mobility at Forefront of Diversity Debate," *The Times Special Report*, June 21, 2017.

99. Laura Whateley, "It Is Not Enough to Pat Ourselves on the Back," *The Times Special Report*, June 21, 2017.

100. Social Mobility Foundation, "Social Mobility Employer Index 2018," accessed January 4, 2018, http://www.socialmobility.org.uk/index/.

101. Barber, "New Index Puts Social Mobility at Forefront of Diversity Debate."

102. Mark Frary, "Blind CVs Help to Reduce Bias," *The Times Special Report*, June 21, 2017.

103. Virginia Matthews, "More Cracks Beginning to Appear in the Class Ceiling," *The Times Special Report*, June 21, 2017.

Rule 7: Strategically Self-Promote

104. Dan Schawbel, *Me 2.0: 4 Steps to Building Your Future* (New York: Kaplan Publishing, 2010), 129–31.

105. For more self-promotion strategies on how to develop your story and deliver it with conviction, read *BRAG! The Art of Tooting Your Own Horn without Blowing It*, by Peggy Klaus.

Rule 8: Be Mindful of Work-Life Integration

106. Shawn Achor and Michelle Gielan, "Resilience Is About How You Recharge, Not How You Endure," *Harvard Business Review*, June 24, 2016, accessed January 4, 2018, https://hbr.org/2016/06/resilience-is-about-how-you-recharge-not-how-you-endure.

107. Silvia Bellezza, Neeru Paharia, and Anat Keinan, "Conspicuous Consumption of Time: When Busyness and Lack of Leisure Time Become a Status Symbol," *Journal of Consumer Research* 44(1) (2017): 118–38, doi:10.1093/jcr/ucw076.

108. Judith K. Sluiter, Allard J. van der Beek, and Monique H. Frings-Dresen, "The Influence of Work Characteristics on the Need for Recovery and Experienced Health: A Study on Coach Drivers," *Ergonomics* 42(4) (1999): 573–83, doi:10.1080/001401399185487.

109. Robert M. Sapolsky, *Why Zebras Don't Get Ulcers* (New York: Holt Paperbacks, 2004), 1–18.

110. Fred R. H. Zijlstra, Mark Cropley, and Leif W. Rydstedt, "From Recovery to Regulation: An Attempt to Reconceptualize 'Recovery from Work,'" *Stress and Health* 30(3) (2014): 244–52, doi: 10.1002/smi.2604.

111. Shawn Achor, "Are the People Who Take Vacations the Ones Who Get Promoted?" *Harvard Business Review*, June 12, 2015, accessed January 4, 2018, https://hbr.org/2015/06/are-the-people-who-take-vacations-the-ones-who-get-promoted.

112. Tom Rath, *Eat Move Sleep: How Small Choices Lead to Big Changes* (Arlington, VA: Missionday, 2013), 21–2, 36–8.

113. Chris Crowley and Henry S. Lodge, *Younger Next Year: A Guide to Living Like 50 Until You're 80 and Beyond* (New York: Workman Publishing, 2004), 33–45, 305.

114. Rachel Bachman, "Five Secrets of Steady Exercisers," *Wall Street Journal*, May 22, 2017, accessed January 4, 2018, http://online.wsj.com/public/resources/documents/print/WSJ_-A015-20170522.pdf.

115. Ronald C. Kessler, Patricia A. Berglund, Catherine Coulouvrat, Goeran Hajak, Thomas Roth, Victoria Shahly, Alicia C. Shillington, Judith J. Stephenson, and James K. Walsh, "Insomnia and the Performance of US Workers: Results from the America Insomnia Survey," *Sleep* 34(9) (2011): 1161–71, doi: 10.5665/SLEEP.1230.

116. For a more extensive compilation of tips on and fun facts about exercise, read *The First 20 Minutes: Surprising Science Reveals How We Can Exercise Better, Train Smarter, Live Longer* by Gretchen Reynolds. Reynolds uses science to debunk myths and set the record straight on best practices when it comes to exercise.

117. Justin Talbot-Zorn and Leigh Marz, "The Busier You Are, the More You Need Quiet Time," *Harvard Business Review*, March 17, 2017, accessed January 4, 2018, https://hbr.org/2017/03/the-busier-you-are-the-more-you-need-quiet-time.

118. Joshua D. Rooks, Alexandra B. Morrison, Merissa Goolsarran, Scott L. Rogers, and Amishi P. Jha, "'We Are Talking about Practice': The Influence of Mindfulness vs. Relaxation Training on Athletes' Attention and Well-Being over High-Demand Intervals," *Journal of Cognitive Enhancement* 1(2) (2017): 141–53, doi: 10.1007/s41465-017-0016-5.

119. Ashley V. Whillans, Elizabeth W. Dunn, Paul Smeets, Rene Bekkers, and Michael I. Norton, "Buying Time Promotes Happiness," *Proceedings of the National Academy of Sciences* 114(32) (2017): 8523–27, doi:10.1073/pnas.1706541114.

120. Ibid.

121. LeanIn.Org and McKinsey & Company, "Women in the Workplace 2016," accessed January 4, 2018, https://womenintheworkplace.com/2016.

122. Ibid.

Rule 9: Become a Power Player and Pay It Forward

123. Clint Smith, "The Danger of Silence," TED.com, July 2014, accessed January 4, 2018, https://www.ted.com/talks/clint_smith_the_danger_of_silence/transcript.

Rule 10: Maintain Career Flexibility

124. Amy Gallo, "You've Made a Mistake. Now What?" *Harvard Business Review*, April 28, 2010, accessed January 4, 2018, https://hbr.org/2010/04/youve-made-a-mistake-now-what.

125. Dan Ciampa, "The More Senior Your Job Title, the More You Need to Keep a Journal," *Harvard Business Review*, July 7, 2017, accessed January 4, 2018, https://hbr.org/2017/07/the-more-senior-your-job-title-the-more-you-need-to-keep-a-journal.

Made in the USA
San Bernardino, CA
01 August 2018